THE ART OF WOODWORKING

WOODEN TOYS AND CRAFTS

THE ART OF WOODWORKING

WOODEN TOYS AND CRAFTS

TIME-LIFE BOOKS
ALEXANDRIA, VIRGINIA

ST. REMY PRESS
MONTREAL • NEW YORK

THE ART OF WOODWORKING was produced by
ST. REMY PRESS

PUBLISHER	Kenneth Winchester
PRESIDENT	Pierre Léveillé
Series Editor	Pierre Home-Douglas
Series Art Director	Francine Lemieux
Senior Editor	Marc Cassini
Editor	Andrew Jones
Art Directors	Normand Boudreault, Luc Germain, Michel Giguère
Designers	Hélène Dion, Jean-Guy Doiron, François Daxhelet, François Longpré
Picture Editor	Christopher Jackson
Writers	John Dowling, David Simon
Research Assistant	Adam Van Sertima
Contributing Illustrators	Gilles Beauchemin, Michel Blais, Ronald Durepos, Michael Stockdale, James Thérien
Administrator	Natalie Watanabe
Production Manager	Michelle Turbide
System Coordinator	Eric Beaulieu
Photographer	Robert Chartier
Administrative Assistant	Dominique Gagné
Proofreader	Garet Markvoort
Indexer	Christine M. Jacobs

Time-Life Books is a division of Time Life Inc.,
a wholly owned subsidiary of
THE TIME INC. BOOK COMPANY

TIME-LIFE INC.

President and CEO	John M. Fahey
Editor-in-Chief	John L. Papanek

TIME-LIFE BOOKS

President	John D. Hall
Vice-President, Director of Marketing	Nancy K. Jones
Managing Editor	Roberta Conlan
Director of Design	Michael Hentges
Director of Editorial Operations	Ellen Robling
Consulting Editor	John R. Sullivan
Vice-President, Book Production	Marjann Caldwell
Production Manager	Marlene Zack
Quality Assurance Manager	James King

THE CONSULTANTS

Giles Miller-Mead taught advanced cabinetmaking at Montreal technical schools for more than ten years. A native of New Zealand, he has worked as a restorer of antique furniture.

Fred Sneath is a retired educator who builds articulated wooden toys and early musical instruments in Stony Creek, Ontario. His work has been highlighted in *Fine Woodworking* and *Continuo* magazines.

Chester Van Ness designs and builds wooden toys in his Scotland, Ontario, studio. He also builds children's activity centers for hospitals and doctors' offices and designs dust removal systems for small workshops.

Wooden toys & crafts
 p. cm. — (The Art of woodworking)
Includes index.
ISBN 0-8094-9529-5
1. Wooden toy making. Time-Life Books. II. Title: Wooden toys and crafts. III. Series.
TT174.5.W6W65 1995
745.592—dc20   94-24187
                                              CIP

For information about any Time-Life book,
please call 1-800-621-7026, or write:
Reader Information
Time-Life Customer Service
P.O. Box C-32068
Richmond, Virginia
23261-2068

CONTENTS

Steve Malavolta on
HAND-CUT WOODEN PUZZLES

My interest in woodworking has a lot to do with wood itself, which offers a stunning variety of colors, different cutting and shaping abilities, and a wide range of tactile qualities. In the beginning of my career I explored these properties by making lap dulcimers and guitars, incorporating a good amount of inlay. With holiday gift-making being a tradition of mine, I once made a stand-up serpent puzzle for my nephew. It was the start of a new career and what I sometimes consider an obsession.

My earliest puzzles were only nicely colored and figured slabs of wood, cut into somewhat undefined pieces and then framed. Currently I am incorporating my inlay skills in a style similar to intarsia, creating three-dimensional architectural puzzles, abstracts, and landscapes like the one shown on page 108. (The inlay work, along with the cutting of the puzzle pieces, is done on a scroll saw with a jewelers blade.) All of my woods are hand-picked for consistency of grain, color, and figure. These qualities lead me as a designer into creating the individual piece.

There are a few properties that I always keep in mind when making what I consider to be a good puzzle. First, the design needs to be visually pleasing. Then comes the challenge. The complexity of the puzzle can range from the simple to the mind-boggling. In all my pieces I use a standard-shaped puzzle piece with a well-defined lobe and socket on each side to lock it to the others, a process that carries through the whole puzzle. After years of freehand cutting, this is a process that has become second nature, and I find this part of my work to be very meditative.

Layering adds a unique touch to my puzzles. It not only creates depth for the design but also increases the puzzle's difficulty. Because the woods are kept in their natural colors, it enables me to finish the pieces on both sides, making solving the puzzle even harder. Finishing is also an important part of my puzzles, as they are meant to be handled, giving them a tactile as well as a visual appeal.

Each puzzle is made to be played, creating both entertainment and intellectual challenge. I take pleasure in knowing that through the years I have been able to combine both elements in each piece. My goal as a woodworker is to present my puzzles as enjoyable, playable works of art of heirloom quality. My recommendation to you is to practice your woodworking techniques and enjoy the pleasures that the process of creating and the use of the finished piece gives back to you.

Steve Malavolta is a self-taught woodworker who has been designing brain-twisting, hand-cut wooden jigsaw puzzles since 1977. He also makes letter openers and sculptural lighting fixtures at Different Grains, his Albuquerque, New Mexico studio.

Don Buhler builds

A GLIDING ROCKING HORSE

B uilding a rocking horse was more than a way to keep busy on long winter evenings. It was the fulfillment of a dream that I had cherished for years before I was a father. My wife, Darlene, and I have been blessed with one son, Nathan, and one daughter, Melissa. Nathan's first birthday present was to be a rocking horse, hand-made by his dad.

As his birthday drew near, I started the project and soon found that Nathan was engrossed with the building process itself. So I took him to my shop every night where he watched me from his stroller. Hour after hour, he jabbered away and watched intently until the magic moment each evening when his eyes became too heavy to stay open. After he fell asleep it was I who enjoyed looking at him, inspired by his presence. Creating something is rewarding in itself, but creating something for your own child is a special treat.

The concept of a glider rocking horse came from observing the silky-smooth, silent action of glider rocking chairs. The glider rocker is easy for small tots to get moving on all types of floors. The one concern that I had, though, was that the scissor action of the swing-arms could prove dangerous for a young child. This prompted me to incorporate minimum clearances between the swing-arms and the parts next to them into my design. Several times throughout the project I dis-carded and re-did the parts to make sure everything was absolutely right.

The part of the project that I enjoyed the most was carving the shape of the horse, especially the head. This is where the horse took on "life." The parts that Nathan enjoyed were the final touches—the painting, the saddle, and the halter. This made it look like a real horse that would be fun to ride.

I managed to finish the horse in time for Nathan's birthday, and he loved it. He rode his horse every day and proudly told anyone who asked that "My Daddy made it for me." Over months and then years, Nathan continued to ride his pony. At about eight months of age, Melissa joined in the fun.

The horse has been ridden and enjoyed inside and outside our home for seven years now and will always be cherished as part of our family memories. Somehow when you build a toy for your child, it is so different than just buying one. Happy building!

Don Buhler is a full-time woodworker who runs Swan Valley Cabinet Works in Swan River, Manitoba.

Johannes Michelsen tips his
TURNED HAT

After years of turning bowls and vases in my spare time, I started to search for a different sort of project, and hit on the idea of turning head wear. Being busy with life, I didn't seize upon the idea immediately but instead treated it as a joke, putting bowls and vases on my head and calling them hats. Then late in 1990 my wife and I were invited to a wedding with a country and western theme, and we were asked to dress accordingly. This was the catalyst I needed. I figured that if I didn't do "The Hat" for this occasion I probably never would. I chose a piece of black cherry and turned a diameter large enough to fit the front-to-back measurement of my head. This first effort lacked the grace of the hats I turn today, but was well received despite its lack of true hat form.

My own head, being fairly round as averages go—6¾ by 8 inches—was quite easy to replicate in my first attempts at bending freshly turned hats. Yet as I became familiar with more heads I encountered more ovalness, some as much as 2½ inches out of round. Studying the type and degree of distortion from various woods and the different orientation of the bowls in the log led me to the idea that I could turn the hats green, conceivably using shrinkage and natural distortion to achieve a better fit. It turned out this was not enough, and around hat number 50 I decided to use force to encourage more shape. This was done with 18-inch-long wood springs and threaded rods clamped to the sides of the hat.

To get a custom fit I measure the head with a lead-filled "Curvex" ruler, and transfer the shape to paper. Measuring front to back and side to side, I came up with an average for the hat size. To this I add a sufficient amount to compensate for shrinkage, and then turned the resulting diameter. I form the hat from a native northern hardwood—maple, ash, butternut, walnut, or yellow birch—down to a final thickness of about 3⁄32 inches, slightly thicker at the edge of the brim and the band for strength, and thinner everywhere else for bendability and lightness. The bands are done by pressing a thin piece of exotic wood against the hat as it spins. Ebony gives black; rosewood, red; padauk, burnt orange; and so on. I clamp the hat for several days to attain the two major dimensions. Once dry in its custom-fitted shape, it is sanded and sprayed with 12-15 coats of acrylic lacquer for durability and weatherability.

The appeal of wood hats is apparently broad. I have customers across the country and in Europe. They range from a cotton farmer in Louisiana who likes to wear her derby on crop inspection trips to Hollywood personalities, and of course turned wood collectors everywhere. The future for turned hats looks bright indeed.

Johannes Michelsen is a wood turner who once turned a cane with a miniature, battery-powered lathe that served as the handle. He operates a studio in Manchester Center, Vermont.

TOYS AND CRAFTS BASICS

Most of the requirements for building furniture—functional designs, proper tool setups and techniques, and safe work habits—are also crucial to making toys and crafts. But wooden toys, because they are intended for use by children, involve other considerations. Foremost among these is safety. As shown below, toys intended for infants and toddlers have to be large enough that they cannot be swallowed and lodge in a child's windpipe. And since children explore as much with their mouths as with their hands, the wood species you use for your projects and the finish you apply—whether paint or a clear finish—must be non-toxic. The charts on page 13 rate the toxicity of various finishes and wood species.

Because many toys are made with turned parts, many of which are small, the lathe and scroll saw are two of the most commonly used tools. This chapter also explains how to set up both machines and provides information on some basic operations and techniques.

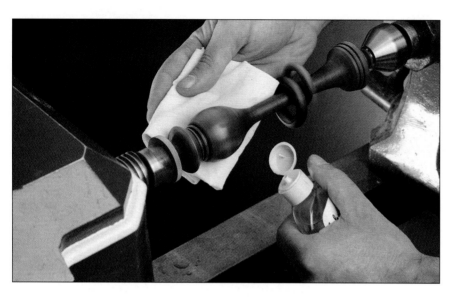

A coating of baby oil is applied to a child's rattle with a cloth while the toy is spinning on a lathe. Toys designed for children must be finished with a nontoxic product. Baby oil, which is actually scented mineral oil, is one of the safest.

MAKING CHILD-SAFE TOYS

Checking toys for size

If you are making a toy for an infant or toddler, you must ensure that neither the toy nor any detachable parts is so small that the child could swallow the piece and choke on it. The simple jig shown at right, consisting of a wood block with an oval hole drilled through it, will help you determine whether a toy is sized properly. Mark the width of the oval—1⅜ inch—by drawing two parallel lines across the board. Then adjust a compass to one-half this measurement and draw two circles within the lines so the oval opening formed by the circles will be 1¹⁵⁄₁₆ inches long. Drill out the opening. If any part of a toy, like the rattle shown, can pass through the hole, it is unsafe for a young child.

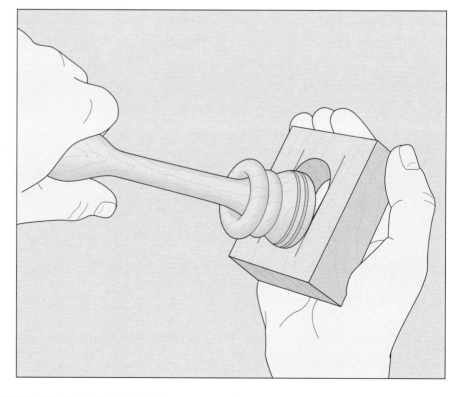

CHILD-SAFE FINISHES

SAFE FINISHES	
Baby oil	Penetrating
Mineral oil	Penetrating
Beeswax	Surface
Shellac	Surface
Paraffin wax	Surface
Raw linseed oil	Penetrating
Pure tung oil	Penetrating

SAFE FINISHES	
Pure walnut oil	Penetrating
Carnauba wax	Surface
Non-toxic paint with the seal of the Arts and Crafts Materials Institute or the words "conforms to the ASTMD-4236"	Surface
Modeler's enamel paint	Surface

The chart above lists wood finishes that are considered safe for toys that children may put into their mouths. Refrain from using any other product—even if it is labeled as being nontoxic or the Materials Safety Data Sheet compiled for the product (available from the manufacturer) does not include any toxic substances. A toxin must be present in concentrations greater than 1 percent to be listed, and many such substances, such as metallic driers added to finishes, usually comprise less than 1 percent. Even after a finish is fully cured, rough handling can cause a small portion of the finish to flake off and be ingested. As a result, any toxic ingredient in a finishing product is potentially harmful. After applying a finish, make sure that the surface is completely dry before giving the toy to a child. Paints that are safe once fully dry may give off harmful volatiles as they cure. And do not assume that a paint or finish is completely cured when it is dry to the touch. Some products can take months to cure completely; refer to the label instructions for drying times. The chart also distinguishes between products that penetrate the wood or simply remain on the surface.

TOXIC WOODS

TOXIC WOODS	
Arbor vitae	R
Black spruce	R S
Boxwood	R S
California redwood	R S T
Cashew	S
Cocobolo	R S
Ebony	R S T
European larch	R S

TOXIC WOODS	
European spruce	R S
Imbuia	R S
Iroko	R S
Lacewood	R S
Mahogany	R S
Pine	R S
Red cedar	R S
Rosewood	R S

TOXIC WOODS	
Satinwood, Ceylon	S
Silky-oak	R S
Teak	R S
Wenge	R S
Western red cedar	R S T
R= Respiratory ailments S= Skin and eye irritations T= Toxic effects	

The dust from many wood species can pose health risks ranging from respiratory ailments to skin and eye irritations. Some woods contain chemicals that can cause toxic effects. The chart above lists a number of species and their possible health effects.

LATHE BASICS

The lathe shown below is a typical freestanding model that will serve you well for most toy-making projects. Lathe size is measured in two ways: swing and capacity. Swing is twice the distance between the headstock spindle and the bed, which limits the diameter of blanks.

Capacity is the distance between the headstock and tailstock, which limits the length of blanks. The weight of a lathe is important, as greater weight provides more stability and dampens vibration. Another feature to consider is how easy it is to change speeds; larger workpieces

must be turned at lower speeds than smaller ones. Changing the speeds of some lathes involves switching a drive belt between two sets of stepped pulleys; other models have variable-speed pulley systems that allow the speed to be changed without switching off the tool.

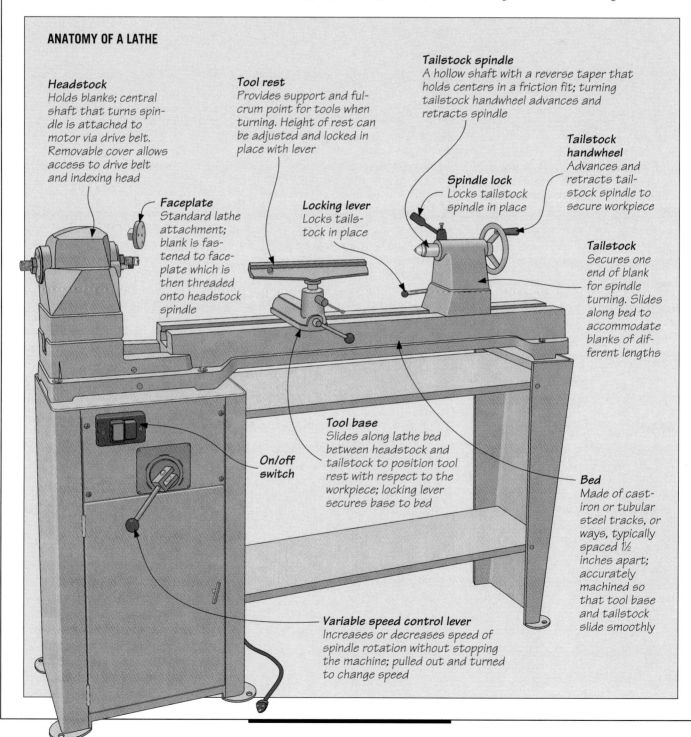

ANATOMY OF A LATHE

Headstock
Holds blanks; central shaft that turns spindle is attached to motor via drive belt. Removable cover allows access to drive belt and indexing head

Faceplate
Standard lathe attachment; blank is fastened to faceplate which is then threaded onto headstock spindle

Tool rest
Provides support and fulcrum point for tools when turning. Height of rest can be adjusted and locked in place with lever

Locking lever
Locks tailstock in place

Tailstock spindle
A hollow shaft with a reverse taper that holds centers in a friction fit; turning tailstock handwheel advances and retracts spindle

Spindle lock
Locks tailstock spindle in place

Tailstock handwheel
Advances and retracts tailstock spindle to secure workpiece

Tailstock
Secures one end of blank for spindle turning. Slides along bed to accommodate blanks of different lengths

On/off switch

Tool base
Slides along lathe bed between headstock and tailstock to position tool rest with respect to the workpiece; locking lever secures base to bed

Bed
Made of cast-iron or tubular steel tracks, or ways, typically spaced 1½ inches apart; accurately machined so that tool base and tailstock slide smoothly

Variable speed control lever
Increases or decreases speed of spindle rotation without stopping the machine; pulled out and turned to change speed

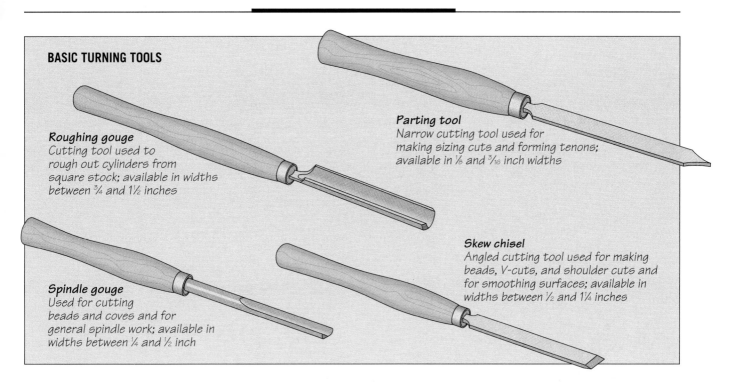

BASIC TURNING TOOLS

Roughing gouge
Cutting tool used to rough out cylinders from square stock; available in widths between ¾ and 1½ inches

Parting tool
Narrow cutting tool used for making sizing cuts and forming tenons; available in ⅛ and 3⁄16 inch widths

Spindle gouge
Used for cutting beads and coves and for general spindle work; available in widths between ¼ and ½ inch

Skew chisel
Angled cutting tool used for making beads, V-cuts, and shoulder cuts and for smoothing surfaces; available in widths between ½ and 1¼ inches

TURNING A CYLINDER

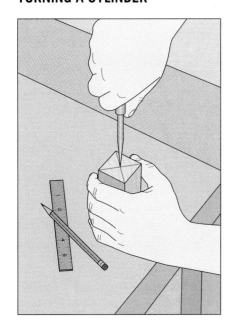

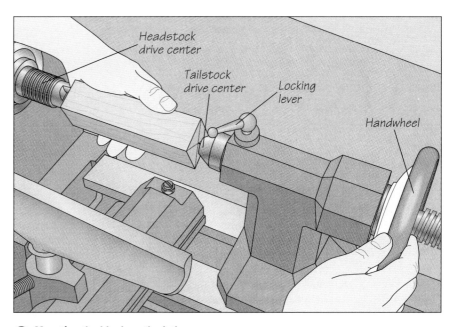

1 Marking the centers of the blank
To mount a blank between centers on the lathe, mark two lines across each end from corner to corner. The lines will intersect at the center. Next, use an awl to make indentations at both points (above).

2 Mounting the blank on the lathe
Butt one end of the blank against the tailstock's live center. Supporting the other end of the blank with one hand, slide the tailstock toward the headstock until the drive center in the headstock aligns with the indentation you made in step 1. Secure the tailstock in place with the locking lever and advance the the tailstock spindle and center by turning the handwheel until the blank is held firmly between the centers (above). Secure the tailstock spindle in place with the spindle lock.

3 Turning a cylinder

Holding a roughing gouge with a overhand grip, brace the blade on the tool rest. Cut very lightly into the blank, making sure that the bevel is rubbing against the stock and moving the gouge smoothly along the tool rest. The gouge will begin rounding the corners of the workpiece. The smoothest cuts are made by moving the blade with the grain. Continue making successively deeper passes along the blank, raising the handle of the tool with each pass, until the edges are completely rounded and you have a cylinder *(right)*. Adjust the position of the tool rest as you progress to keep it as close to the blank as possible.

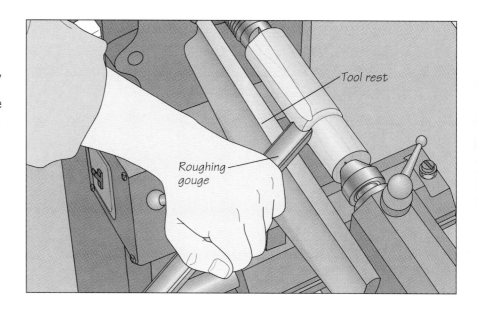

MAKING COVES AND BEADS

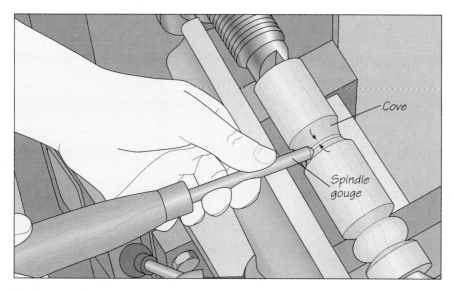

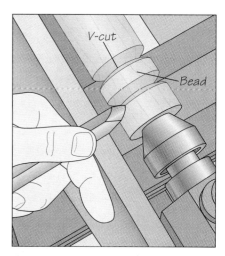

Turning a cove

Outline the cove on the blank with a pencil. Then, hold a spindle gouge in an underhand grip with the flute pointing sideways and slice into the wood just inside one of the marked lines with only the cutting edge of the tool. Slowly angle the tool handle back towards the line until the bevel rubs on the workpiece, and make a scooping cut down to the middle of the cove. As you make the cut, turn the handle to rotate the bevel against the workpiece. The gouge should be flat on its back when it reaches the center of the cove. Make the second cut from the opposite side of the cove. Work in a downhill direction, as shown by the arrows—from a high point to a low point on the blank; never cut uphill or against the grain, otherwise the tool will dig into the wood. Repeat the process from both sides of the cove, keeping the bevel rubbing on the stock at all times *(above)*. Continue cutting back to the marked lines until the cove is complete.

Turning a bead

A skew chisel enables you to turn beads with sharp detail. Outline the bead on the stock with a pencil, then make a V-cut at each line. For best results, use the long point of the chisel. Then, working on one side of the V-cuts, widen the cut, slowly lifting the handle so the bevel rubs and the long point of the chisel makes a rounded, rolling cut *(above)*. Repeat for the other side of the bead, making sure your cuts are always made in a downhill direction. Once the shape of the bead is smooth, turn a round shoulder on each side of the bead.

SCROLL SAW BASICS

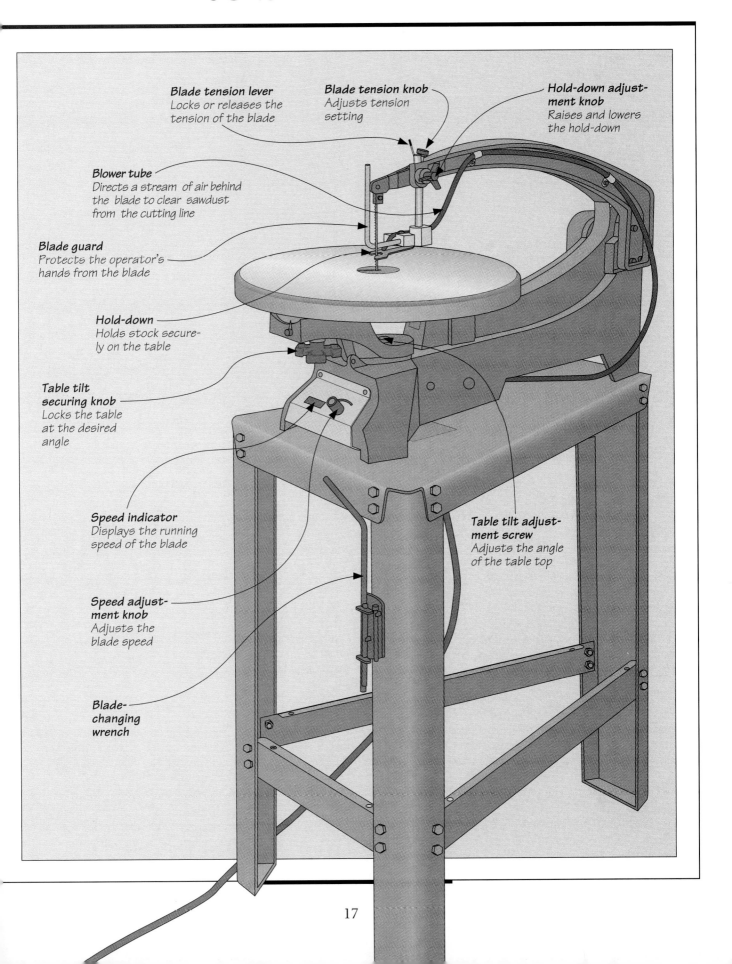

Blade tension lever
Locks or releases the tension of the blade

Blade tension knob
Adjusts tension setting

Hold-down adjustment knob
Raises and lowers the hold-down

Blower tube
Directs a stream of air behind the blade to clear sawdust from the cutting line

Blade guard
Protects the operator's hands from the blade

Hold-down
Holds stock securely on the table

Table tilt securing knob
Locks the table at the desired angle

Speed indicator
Displays the running speed of the blade

Speed adjustment knob
Adjusts the blade speed

Blade-changing wrench

Table tilt adjustment screw
Adjusts the angle of the table top

BLADE GAUGES AND THEIR USES

BLADE TYPES
Standard scroll blade *A coarse-cutting blade usually used for cutting thick or hard stock; has teeth similar to those on a handsaw. Some have pins on the ends, requiring a larger hole for inside cuts*
Skip-tooth fret blade *Ideal for cutting finer details; the skip-tooth design allows sawdust to clear, reducing friction and heat*
Spiral blade *A standard blade twisted to cut in all directions without turning the stock; requires greater skill for precise cuts because it produces a wider kerf than other blades*

GAUGE NUMBER	TEETH PER INCH	USES
2/0 0 1	28 25 23	For intricate work and thin stock. Good for veneers and materials such as hard plastics and thin ($\frac{1}{16}$- to $\frac{3}{32}$-inch) materials
2 3 4	20 18 15	For cutting tight radiuses in thin ($\frac{3}{32}$- to $\frac{1}{8}$-inch) stock, veneers, and plastics
5 6	14 13	For cutting tight radiuses in thicker ($\frac{1}{8}$ inch or more) materials, hard and soft-woods, and plastics
7 8 9 10 11 12	12 11.5 11.5 11 9.5 9.5	For cutting wood thicker than $\frac{3}{16}$ inch

MAKING AN INSIDE CUT

1 Preparing the workpiece
Since a scroll saw blade is detachable, you can bore a hole through the waste area of your workpiece and slip the blade through the hole. Make sure the hole is large enough to accommodate the blade. Detach the blade, set the workpiece on the saw table with the hole centered over the table opening, and feed the blade up through the hole *(right)*.

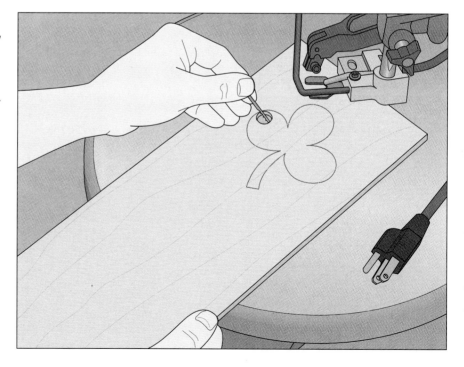

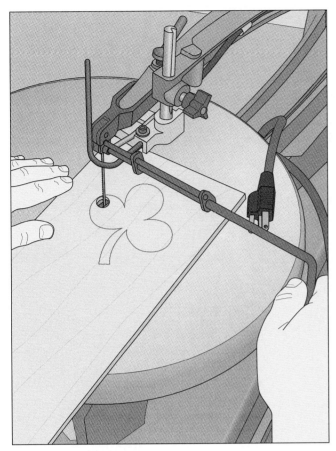

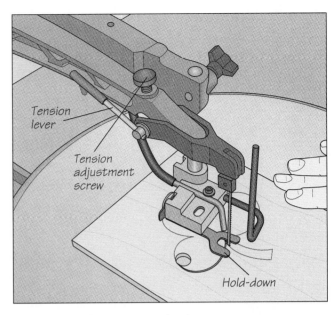

3 Setting up the saw and starting the cut
Check the tension by pushing a board with moderate pressure up against the blade; the blade should deflect about ⅛ inch. To adjust the blade tension, release the tension lever, then turn the tension adjustment screw clockwise to increase tension on the blade and counterclockwise to reduce the tension. Lock the tension lever back into position. As you gain experience, you will be able to pluck the blade and listen for the sound it makes to gauge the tension. Once the blade is properly tensioned, lower the hold-down so that it presses the workpiece firmly against the table. To start the cut, align the blade with the cutting line and feed the workpiece with both hands *(above)*.

2 Reattaching the blade
Slip the end of the blade into the blade clamp mechanism and tighten it with the hex wrench supplied with the machine to secure the blade in position *(above)*.

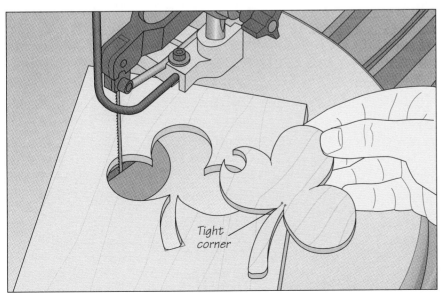

4 Finishing the cut
To cut tight curves pivot the workpiece on the table, shifting your hand position as necessary. For 90° or greater turns, like those at the top of the stem section in the leaf design shown at left, cut slightly beyond the cutting line into the waste section, then pivot the workpiece, and continue along the cutting line. Once you return to your starting point, remove the waste section and detach the blade to free the workpiece.

MODELS

Wheeled vehicles, large and small, have been perennial favorites with children and adults alike for generations. This chapter shows you how to build three wooden models that are based on real-life counterparts: a locomotive, a dump truck, and a tractor-rock picker. As the photo on page 20 confirms, the results are certain to please and delight.

These projects will exercise a range of woodworking skills, from the authentic detailing involved in making the locomotive *(page 22)* and the simple, sturdy construction techniques needed for the dump truck *(page 31)* to the fine shaping of the tractor and rock picker *(page 36)*.

The locomotive is a 1/32-scale model of an early 20th-Century coal-burning steam engine. In addition to making all of its parts to scale, you can use contrasting hardwoods to highlight particular details of the model. The wooden parts of the locomotive shown on page 20 were finished with three coats of satin-finish polyurethane. Clear nail polish was applied to the

The boiler and smoke box of the locomotive shown on page 20 can be turned from a single blank on the lathe. As shown above, the demarcation between the two elements can be burned into the blank with a length of wire fastened to shop-made handles.

brass parts to prevent tarnishing. By adding railroad tracks and ties and displaying the train in a realistic setting, the locomotive can be transformed from toy to exhibit.

The dump truck is a sturdy toy that faithfully recreates the tireless strength of old-style trucks. It is built to withstand even the most punishing "driver" and its spacious box is designed to hold a variety of articles that its young owner might wish to transport. The model featured in this chapter is made with parts that cannot pinch or squeeze a child's hand, like the sloped ends of the lever mechanism *(page 35)*.

The tractor and rock picker come from a long line of rugged farming machinery. With its attention to detail and realistic moving parts, this toy can serve an educational function as well as provide many hours of play.

Whatever type of finish you apply to these vehicles, remember to choose a nontoxic product if you are making the model for a child. Refer to the Toys and Crafts Basics chapter *(page 12)* for more information on child-safe finishes.

Built by Doug Kenney of South Dennis, Massachusetts, the toy train shown at left is a carefully crafted 1/32-scale reproduction of an American Standard steam locomotive in operation at the turn of the 20th Century. To complete the realistic setting, the train is displayed on rails and ties cut from contrasting hardwoods. The rails measure ⅛-by-⁵⁄₁₆ inch; the ties are ¼-by-⁷⁄₁₆-by-3 inches.

LOCOMOTIVE

uilding the engine shown below is essentially a matter of preparing all the parts illustrated on page 23 and gluing them to the chassis. You can cut and assemble or cut all the pieces first, then glue only when all the components are ready. To help you produce a scale model, the profile and dimensions of all the necessary parts are provided. The following pages show step-by-step instructions for producing the more challenging pieces.

Although the locomotive is made mainly from wood, a few items of metal hardware are required. You will need ⅜-inch-long No. 16 brass escutcheon pins, for example, to attach the connecting rods to the wheels. Drill pilot holes for the pins ⁷⁄₁₆ inch from the center of the wheels. The connecting and drive rods are cut from 2⅝-inch-long 0.025-gauge ¼-inch-wide brass strips. The spacing between the holes through each end of the connecting rods should be equal to the distance between the drive wheels: 2⁵⁄₁₆ inches. Make the piston from a 2¼-inch-long, ³⁄₃₂-inch-diameter brass rod with a hook at one end and attach it to the drive rod. Push the piston into a 1⅞ length of ⅛-inch-diameter tubing, then fit the tubing into the cylinder glued to the chassis.

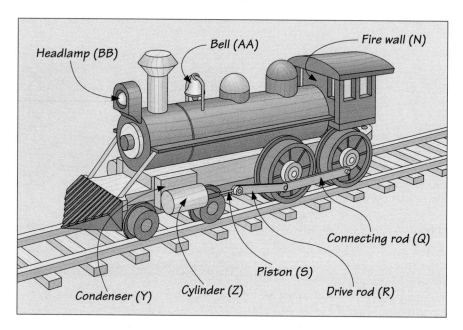

Headlamp (BB) Bell (AA) Fire wall (N) Condenser (Y) Cylinder (Z) Piston (S) Drive rod (R) Connecting rod (Q)

ANATOMY OF A LOCOMOTIVE

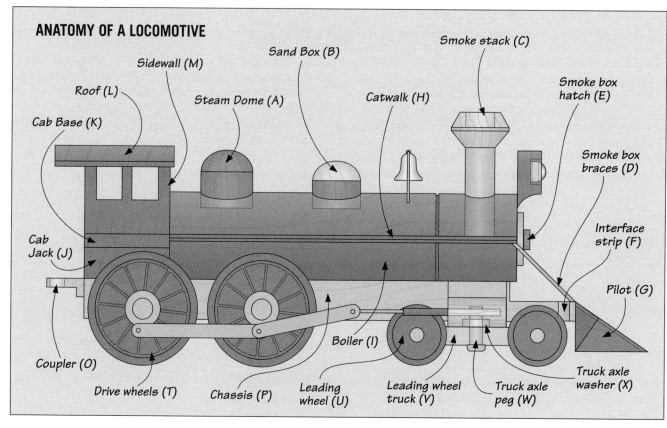

Roof (L) Sidewall (M) Sand Box (B) Smoke stack (C) Cab Base (K) Steam Dome (A) Catwalk (H) Smoke box hatch (E) Smoke box braces (D) Cab Jack (J) Interface strip (F) Pilot (G) Coupler (O) Boiler (I) Truck axle washer (X) Drive wheels (T) Chassis (P) Leading wheel (U) Leading wheel truck (V) Truck axle peg (W)

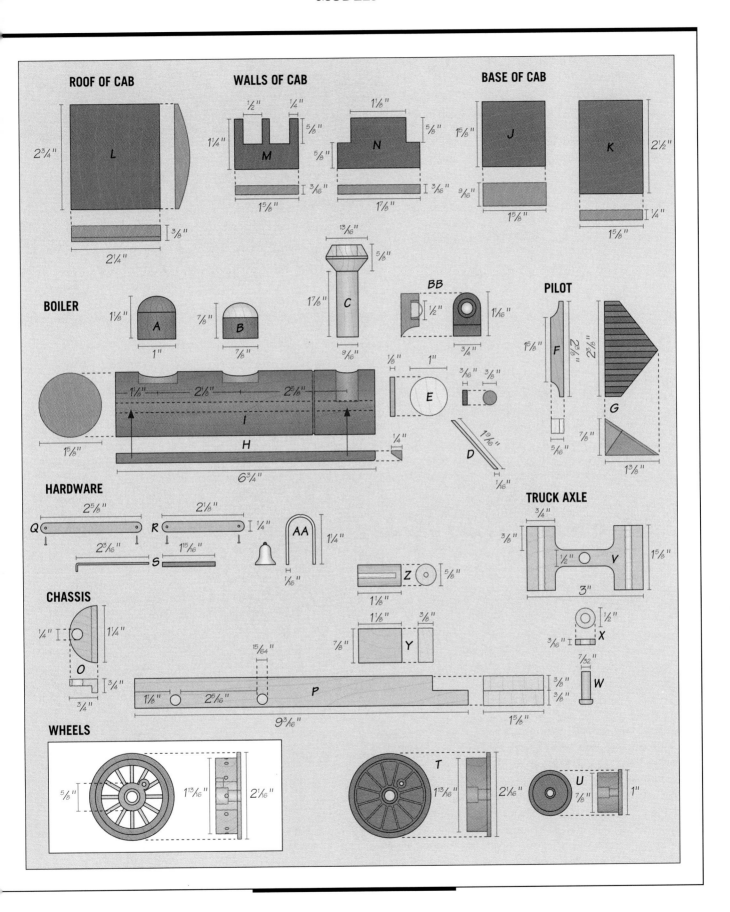

ROOF OF CAB

WALLS OF CAB

BASE OF CAB

BOILER

PILOT

HARDWARE

TRUCK AXLE

CHASSIS

WHEELS

Paired with the shop-made jig shown on page 25, a drill press bores a spoke hole through one of the locomotive's wheels. Consisting of two rings that sandwich the wheel, the jig ensures that the wheels will end up identical. The jig's outer ring features 12 brass bushings spaced equally around its circumference. As a result, the spoke holes will be equidistant around the wheels. After drilling the first hole, insert a dowel or brass rod through the jig rings and the wheel to keep the pieces from rotating as you bore the remaining holes. See detailed instrutions on page 25 for making this jig.

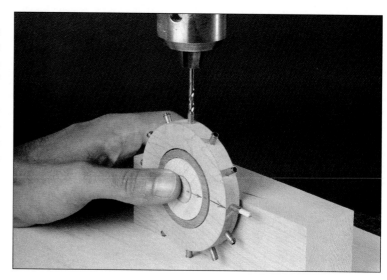

MAKING THE WHEELS

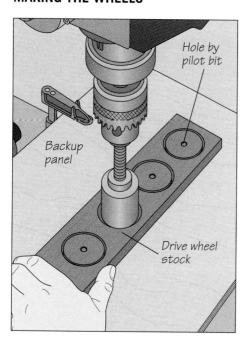

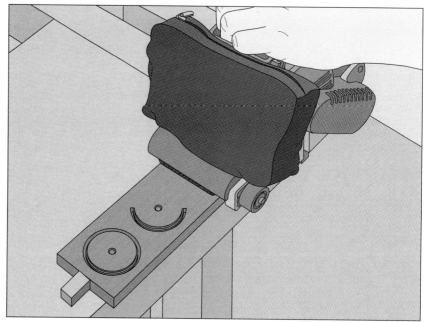

1 Cutting out the wheels

Clamp a backup panel to your drill press table, then prepare the wheel blanks. Cut a ⅝-by-2½-by-15-inch piece of hardwood for the drive wheels and a ⁹⁄₁₆-by-1½-by-8-inch board for the front wheels. Cut both sets of wheels the same way, using one hole saw to define the rim and a smaller hole saw for the flange inside the rim. For the drive wheels, install a 2½-inch hole saw in the drill press and cut four holes in the workpiece, stopping each one ¹⁄₃₂-inch from the underside of the board. Repeat the process with a 2-inch hole saw, aligning the pilot bit with the pilot hole cut by the larger bit *(above, left)*. This will ensure that the flanges are the same width all around the wheel. Follow the same procedure for the front wheels, using 1¼- and 1-inch hole saws. Once all the cuts are made, release the wheels from each blank using a belt sander fitted with an 80-grit sanding belt. Turn over the blank and secure it to the top of your bench. Move the sander back and forth across the surface until it removes enough waste wood to expose the hole saw cuts *(above, right)*. You can now cut imitation spokes into the drive wheels *(step 2)* or use a jig *(page 25)* to construct more detailed drive wheels with spokes made from dowels.

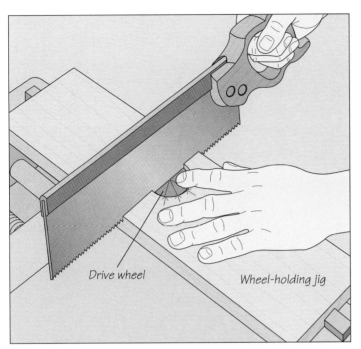

2 Cutting "spokes" into the drive wheels

To create the illusion that the drive wheels are spoked, you can use a backsaw to kerf the outside faces of the wheels. To hold the wheels as you cut them and ensure that the kerfs are spaced equally, use a jig made from a board slightly thicker than the wheels. For the jig, cut a 2½-inch hole into the middle of the board and mark the kerf lines around the circumference of the hole. Spacing the marks 30° apart will allow you to cut 6 kerfs. Secure the jig to your benchtop, insert the wheel in the hole, and transfer the kerf marks onto it. Then holding the wheel in place with an index finger, cut a kerf into the jig and $\frac{1}{16}$ inch into the wheel *(left)*. Keep the saw teeth parallel to the work surface. To cut each remaining kerf, rotate the wheel in the jig until the next kerf mark aligns with the cut in the jig and repeat the cut.

Drive wheel   *Wheel-holding jig*

BUILD IT YOURSELF

A SPOKE-HOLE JIG

The jig shown at right will enable you to make quick work of drilling equidistant holes for spokes around the rim of drive wheels like the ones shown in the photo on page 20. The jig consists of two rings: an outer and inner one. The wheel and hub are held steady for drilling by the two rings; the flange along the wheel's circumference prevents it from slipping out.

Cut the two rings from a board the same thickness as the wheels. Use a 3-inch hole saw to define the outside circumference of the outer ring and a 2-inch hole saw to separate the two rings. Use a ⅝-inch-diameter bit to drill out the hole in the inner ring for the hub; use a short length of dowel for the hub. To prepare the jig, assemble the rings and the hub, and use a $\frac{5}{32}$-inch drill bit to bore holes at 30° intervals through both rings. After drilling the first hole, slip a ⅛-inch dowel into it to keep the rings aligned as you bore the remaining holes. Once all the holes are drilled, insert a piece of brass tubing in each hole in the outer ring, sized to accept a ⅛-inch drill bit. Refer to the color photo on page 24 for instructions on using the jig.

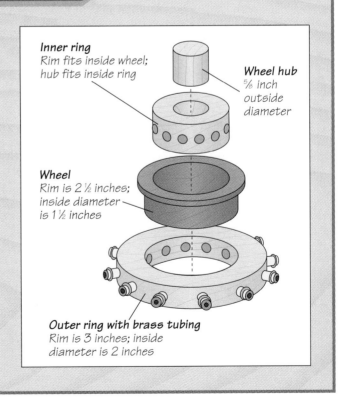

Inner ring
Rim fits inside wheel; hub fits inside ring

Wheel hub
⅝ inch outside diameter

Wheel
Rim is 2½ inches; inside diameter is 1½ inches

Outer ring with brass tubing
Rim is 3 inches; inside diameter is 2 inches

MAKING THE BASE ASSEMBLY

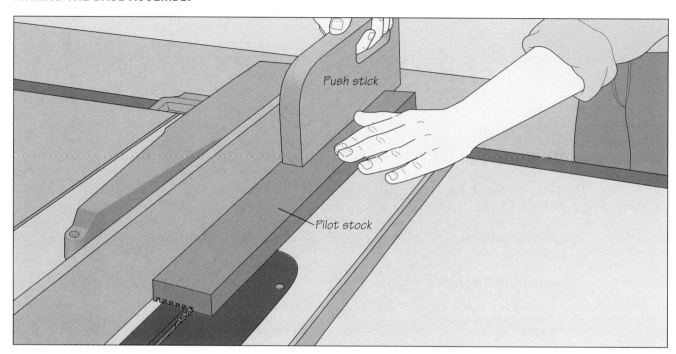

Push stick

Pilot stock

1 Shaping the chassis and the pilot

Refer to the anatomy illustration on page 22 for the dimensions of the locomotive chassis. Cut it to shape on your band saw and remove any marks left by the blade with a sanding block. Make the pilot from a ⅞-by-2½-inch hardwood board, long enough to feed safely across your table saw. To cut the grooves in the pilot, adjust the blade height to ¹⁄₁₆ inch and position the rip fence for a cutting width equal to the width of the blade kerf. Feed the board across the table to cut the first groove, them shift the fence away from the blade by twice the kerf width and repeat. Cut the remaining grooves the same way, feeding the stock with a push stick and pressing the board against the fence at the trailing edge of the stock with your free hand *(above)*. Once all the grooves are cut, saw the pilot to shape on a band saw *(below)*.

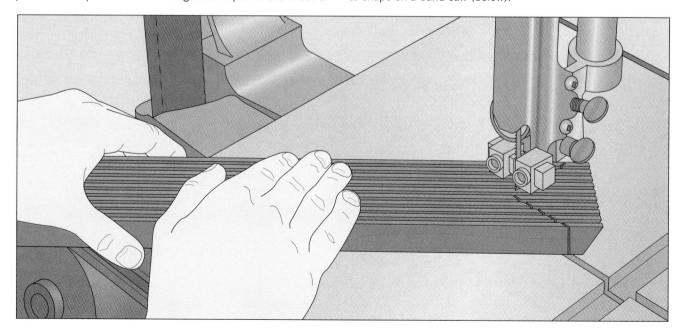

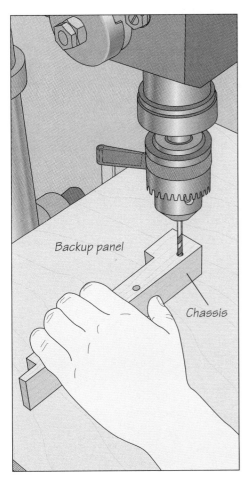

2 Preparing the chassis for the wheels
Clamp a backup panel to your drill press table and install a $^{15}\!/_{64}$-inch bit to bore the axle holes for the drive wheels. Mark the holes 1 inch and 3¼ inches from the back end of the chassis. Then, holding the chassis on its side, drill each hole through the stock *(left)*. Bore matching holes through the wheel hubs or centers.

Backup panel

Chassis

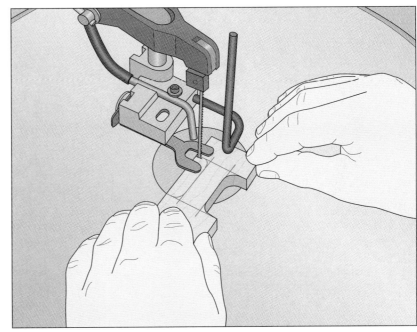

3 Making the truck axle assembly
Refer to the anatomy illustration *(page 22)* for the shape of the truck axle, then cut out the shape on your scroll saw *(above)*. Drill the axle holes in the assembly and front wheels using a $^{3}\!/_{16}$-inch bit. Install the wheels with $^{5}\!/_{32}$-inch-diameter pegs.

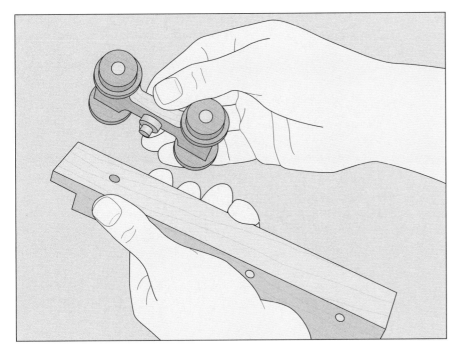

4 Attaching the wheels to the chassis
To mount the front wheels, drill a $^{15}\!/_{64}$-inch-diameter hole into the underside of the chassis near the front end and install the truck assembly with a $^{7}\!/_{32}$-inch peg *(left)*. Also attach the drive wheels to the chassis using $^{7}\!/_{32}$-inch-diameter pegs.

MAKING THE CAB

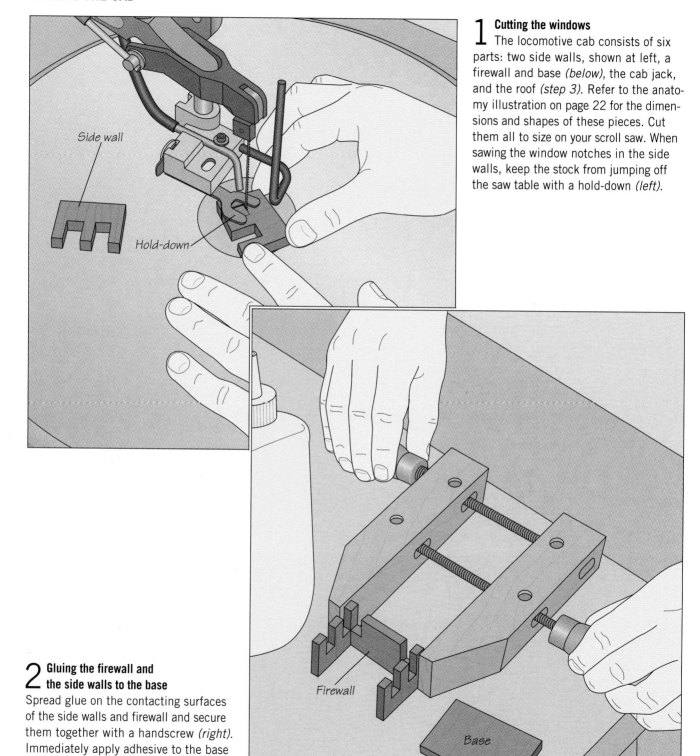

Side wall

Hold-down

Firewall

Base

1 Cutting the windows
The locomotive cab consists of six parts: two side walls, shown at left, a firewall and base *(below)*, the cab jack, and the roof *(step 3)*. Refer to the anatomy illustration on page 22 for the dimensions and shapes of these pieces. Cut them all to size on your scroll saw. When sawing the window notches in the side walls, keep the stock from jumping off the saw table with a hold-down *(left)*.

2 Gluing the firewall and the side walls to the base
Spread glue on the contacting surfaces of the side walls and firewall and secure them together with a handscrew *(right)*. Immediately apply adhesive to the base and set the wall assembly on top, placing a shim under the clamp to keep it level while the glue is curing.

3 Shaping the roof

Make the roof of the cab from a ⅜-by-2¼-by-2¾-inch piece of hardwood. Mark the slope of the roof on the long edge of the stock, then use a disk sander to round over the surface. Holding the edge of the stock flat on the sanding table, rock the top of the roof back and forth across the abrasive disk until you cut to the marked line *(right)*. Once you are satisfied with the shape of the roof, glue it to the rest of the cab and mount the cab to the chassis on top of the cab jack.

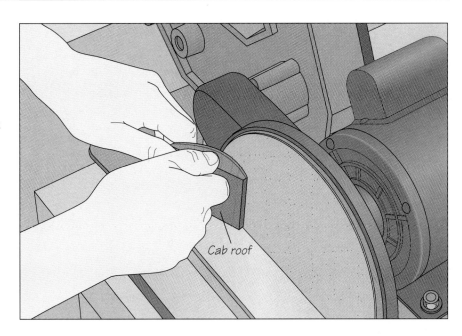

Cab roof

MAKING THE BOILER AND DOMES

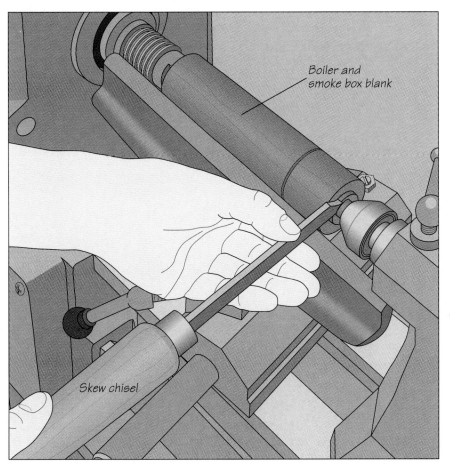

Boiler and smoke box blank

Skew chisel

1 Turning the boiler and smoke box

You can turn the boiler and the 1½-inch-long smoke box separately, using contrasting woods. But if you wish to make them from a single workpiece, mount a 7¼-inch-long blank between centers on your lathe; white ash is a good choice for these parts of the project. Make the blank ½ inch longer if you also want to produce the smoke box hatch from the same blank. Turn the workpiece into a cylinder with a roughing gouge, then use a piece of wire to burn a demarcation line between the boiler and smoke box *(photo, page 21)*. To turn the smoke box hatch down to a diameter of 1 inch and its top down to ¼ inch, use a skew chisel *(left)*. If you are making the hatch separately, use ⅛-inch dowel stock cut from a contrasting hardwood.

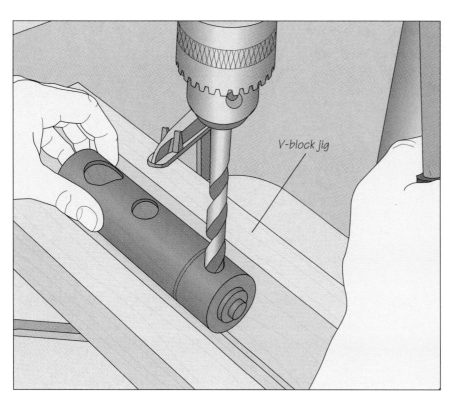

2 Preparing the boiler and smoke box for the stack and domes

Once you have turned the boiler and smoke box, bore the holes for the smoke stack, the steam dome, and sand box on your drill press. Cut a V-shaped wedge out of a wood block, creating a jig that will hold the workpiece steady as you drill the holes. You need to bore three holes with three different bits: one 1⅛ inch in diameter, located 1¼ inch from the back end of the boiler; a second 1 inch in diameter, 2 inches away from the first hole; and a third 9/16 inch in diameter, located ¾ inch from the front end of the smoke box. Hold the workpiece securely in the jig as you drill each hole *(left)*.

3 Making the domes

Shape the domes for the smoke stack, steam dome, and sand box from dowel stock of the correct width. Install a piloted round-over bit in a router and mount the tool in a table. To help you keep the dowel square to the cutter, clamp a pair of guide blocks and a hold-down to the table, as shown at right. Cut a notch out of one end of the hold-down and place it on a shim so the notch will be just above the workpiece and prevent it from jumping up when it contacts the bit. Standing on the right-hand side of the table and holding the dowel against the narrow guide block, advance the workpiece toward the bit. When the dowel contacts the pilot, press it against the block and rotate it toward yourself to shape the end. To finish the dome, simply cut it to length. You can also saw off the dome and glue it to a dowel made from a contrasting hardwood. Once all the domes are made, glue them to the boiler and smoke box.

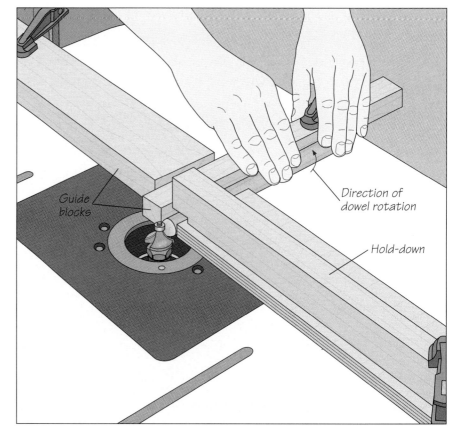

DUMP TRUCK

The truck featured here is an example of a sturdy toy designed with child safety in mind. The moving parts have no pinch points and the truck's surfaces are rounded and smooth. Assembly is fairly straightforward. The quantity and shape of all the parts required are shown below and each can be cut from either solid stock or birch-veneer plywood. All you need to hold the pieces together are a few dowels, although some connections can be reinforced with screws. If you use screws to complete this project, be sure to counterbore the fasteners and cover the heads with wood plugs.

Designed by Chester Van Ness of Scotland, Ontario, the dump truck shown above is built to take abuse and punishment without giving any back. Its corners are rounded and its surfaces are sanded smooth and finished with nontoxic paints.

ANATOMY OF A DUMP TRUCK

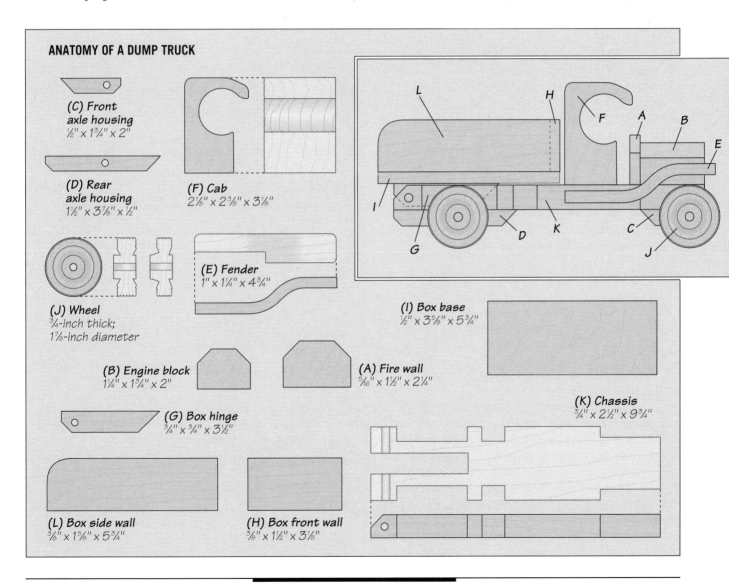

(C) Front axle housing
½" x 1¾" x 2"

(D) Rear axle housing
1½" x 3⅞" x ½"

(F) Cab
2⅛" x 2⅜" x 3⅛"

(J) Wheel
¾-inch thick;
1⅞-inch diameter

(E) Fender
1" x 1¼" x 4¾"

(I) Box base
½" x 3⅝" x 5¾"

(B) Engine block
1¼" x 1¾" x 2"

(A) Fire wall
⁵⁄₁₆" x 1½" x 2¼"

(K) Chassis
¾" x 2½" x 9¾"

(G) Box hinge
¾" x ¾" x 3½"

(L) Box side wall
⅜" x 1⅝" x 5¾"

(H) Box front wall
⅜" x 1½" x 3⅛"

MAKING A DUMP TRUCK

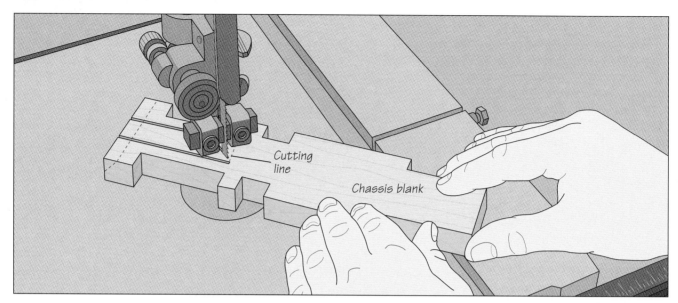

Cutting line

Chassis blank

1 Cutting the chassis and axle housings
Make your chassis blank a little larger than its final dimensions, then use your band saw to cut it to the shape shown in the anatomy illustration *(page 31)*. Outline the profile on the stock, make the cuts on the saw *(above)*, then use a chisel to clean out any corners or edges you could not cut square. To produce the bevel at the back end of the chassis, use the band saw or a stationary power sander, then sand all surfaces smooth. Next, band saw the front and rear axle housings to shape.

2 Preparing the chassis and axle housings for the wheels and box
Mark the holes on the chassis and axle housings for the wheels and the box, then install a ¼-inch bit in your drill press. To minimize tearout as the bit exits the stock, clamp a backup panel to the machine table. Then set the chassis on the panel with the mark aligned under the bit and, holding the workpiece firmly, drill the hole *(right)*. Repeat the process to bore the holes in the axle housings. Since these pieces are too small to hold by hand, clamp them to the backup panel as you drill the holes. You can also bore the holes in the chassis and axle housings before cutting them to shape.

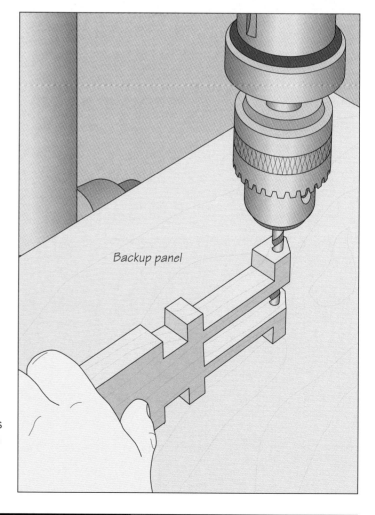

Backup panel

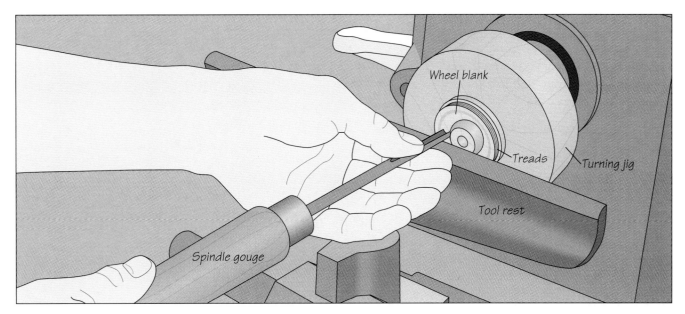

3 Turning the wheels

To produce the wheels on your lathe, start by preparing a simple turning jig on the band saw. Cut the block from 2-inch-thick stock into a 6-inch-diameter circle, then screw it to a faceplate and mount the plate on the lathe headstock. Next, prepare the wheel blanks, cutting them from ¾-inch stock with a 2-inch hole saw mounted on your drill press. Outline one of the wheels in the center of the turning jig, turn on the lathe and use a scraper to cut a ¼-inch-deep recess within the outline.

Seat the blank in the recess, using double-sided tape to hold it in place. You can now turn the blank: Position the tool rest close to the workpiece and use a scraper to cut the treads and then a spindle gouge to shape the recess around the wheel hub *(above)*. Remove the blank from the jig, affix the tape on the side you just turned, and repeat the process to shape the other side of the wheel. Repeat for the other wheels, keeping in mind that the front and back wheels have slightly different profiles *(page 31)*.

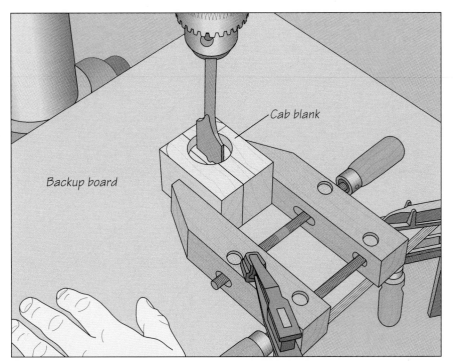

4 Drilling the cab window

Cut your cab blank roughly to size and outline its contours, including the window hole. Locate the hole 1¼ inches from the back end and 2 inches from the bottom of the cab. Install a 1½-inch spade bit in your drill press and clamp a backup panel to the machine table to minimize tearout. Clamp the stock in a handscrew, secure the clamp to the back-up panel so the marked hole is directly under the bit, and drill the hole *(left)*.

5 Shaping the cabin

Cut the contours of the cab on your band saw, feeding the stock with both hands and being careful to keep them clear of the blade *(right)*. Next, cut the fire wall and engine block to shape and sand the pieces.

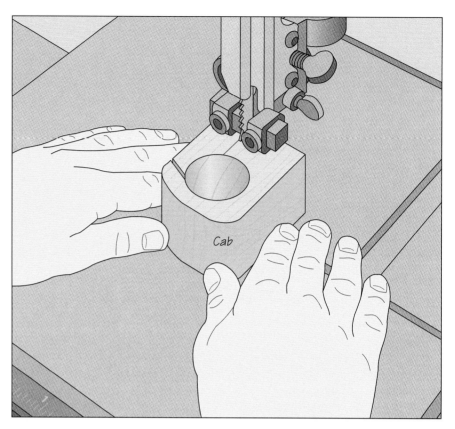

6 Gluing the engine block and cab to the chassis

Start by gluing the cab to the chassis. Once the adhesive has cured, spread glue on the contacting surfaces of the engine block and fire wall, and clamp the pieces together. At the same time, glue the front and rear axle housings to the chassis. Once dry, glue the engine block to the chassis and clamp it in place on a flat work surface, using a wood pad to protect the stock *(below)*.

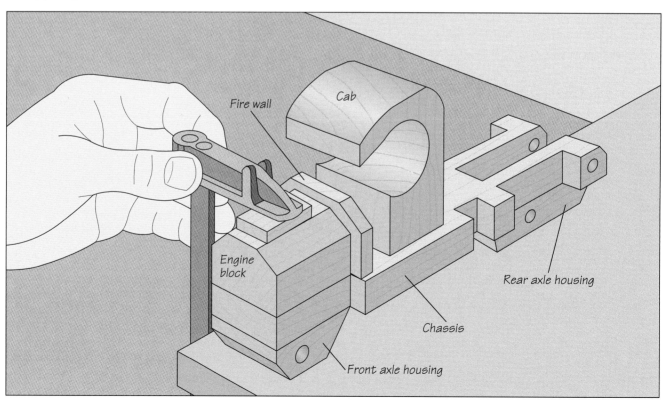

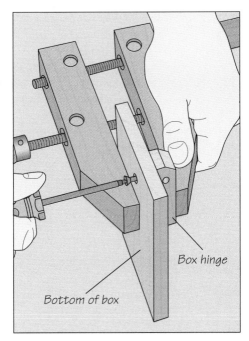

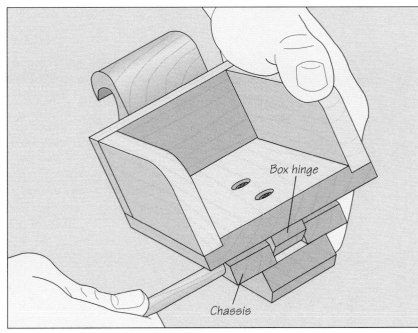

Box hinge

Bottom of box

Box hinge

Chassis

7 Attaching the box to the chassis

Cut the box hinge and the pieces of the box on your band saw, then drill a ¼-inch-diameter hole through the side of the hinge for the dowel that will secure it to the chassis. Screw the hinge to the underside of the box bottom, flush with the back end, using a handscrew to hold the pieces snugly as you drive the screws *(above, left)*. Counterbore the fasteners so you can plug their heads. Next, assemble and glue the box togeth-

er, cutting a shallow rabbet around three sides of the bottom to accept the sides and front. Once the adhesive has cured, place the box on the chassis so the hinge rests in the slot. Dab a little glue on the trailing end of the connecting dowel, then slip the pin through the holes in the chassis and box hinge to secure the box in place *(above, right)*. Conceal the screw heads with wood plugs.

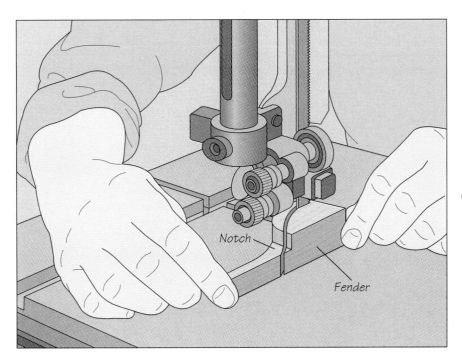

Notch

Fender

8 Mounting the fenders and wheels

Complete the truck by installing the fenders and wheels. Outline the fenders on blanks and cut the pieces to shape on a band saw or scroll saw, starting with the notch on one face, then the curved cut along the edge *(left)*. Glue the fenders in place, then mount the wheels to the axle housings with dowels. You can now finish the truck; be sure to use a child-safe product *(page 12)*.

TRACTOR

Made by Garnet Hall, of Stoughton, Saskatchewan, the tractor and rock picker shown at left straddle the line between toy and display piece. To show off the beauty of the various wood species used, this model was coated with a clear finish. Although the tractor-rock picker can be entirely shop-made, some of the parts, such as the wheels, pegs, and dowels, are available at craft and hobby shops. You can build the toy to scale by cutting the parts according to the full-scale plans provided below and on page 37.

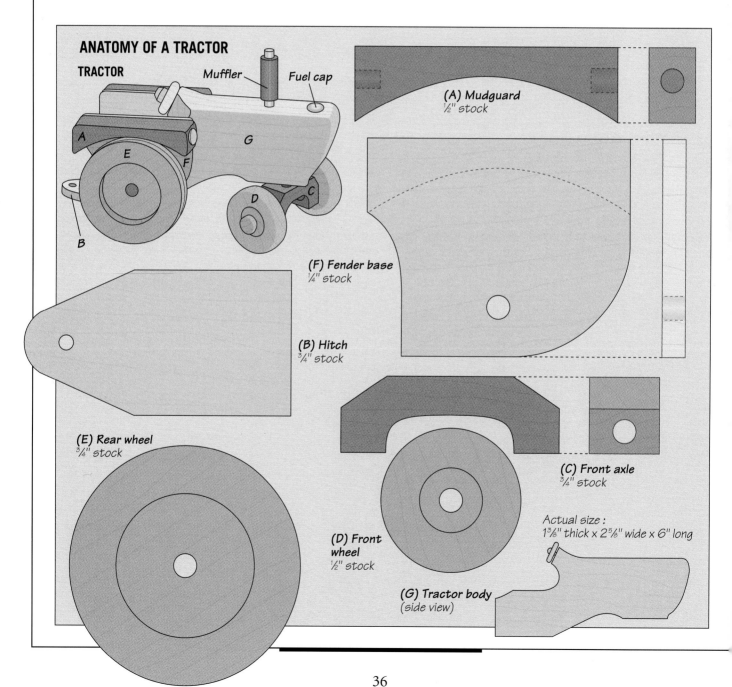

ANATOMY OF A TRACTOR

TRACTOR

Muffler

Fuel cap

A

E

F

G

D

C

B

(A) Mudguard
½" stock

(F) Fender base
¼" stock

(B) Hitch
¾" stock

(E) Rear wheel
¾" stock

(C) Front axle
¾" stock

(D) Front wheel
½" stock

Actual size :
1⅜" thick x 2⅝" wide x 6" long

(G) Tractor body
(side view)

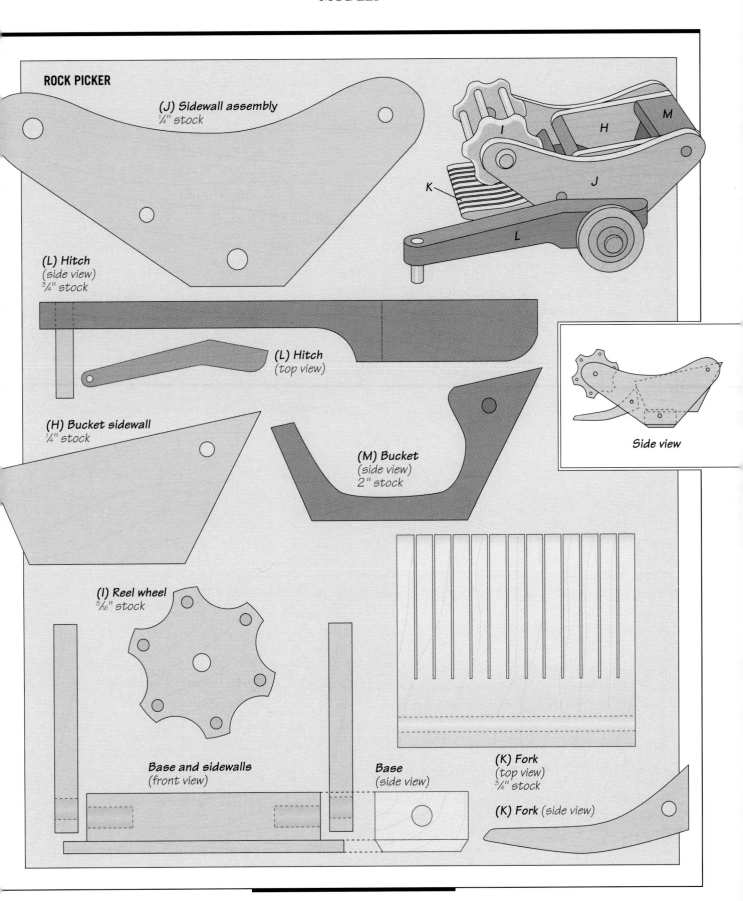

ROCK PICKER

(J) Sidewall assembly
¼" stock

(L) Hitch
(side view)
¾" stock

(L) Hitch
(top view)

(H) Bucket sidewall
¼" stock

(M) Bucket
(side view)
2" stock

Side view

(I) Reel wheel
⁵⁄₁₆" stock

Base and sidewalls
(front view)

Base
(side view)

(K) Fork
(top view)
¾" stock

(K) Fork (side view)

ASSEMBLING THE TRACTOR

1 Shaping the body
Cut the tractor body roughly to size, referring to the anatomy illustration on page 36 for its shape and dimensions. Outline the profile of the body on the stock, cut it out on your band saw, and sand the surfaces smooth. To curve the edges of the body, install a piloted round-over bit in a router and mount the tool in a table. Fashion an auxiliary fence for the infeed side of the table, cutting a notch to cover the bit and rounding the front corner. Screw the fence to a support board and clamp both pieces to the table. Press the stock against the pilot bearing as you feed it across the table. Turn the body over to shape the other side *(right)*. Cut the hitch, drill a hole through it and glue it to the back of the tractor body.

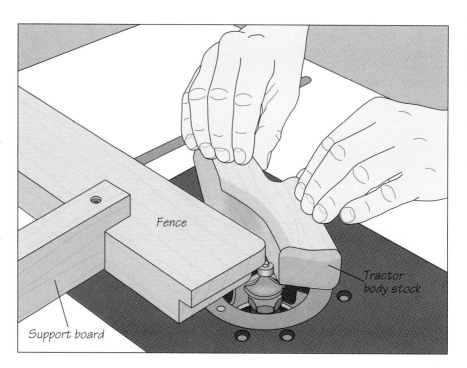

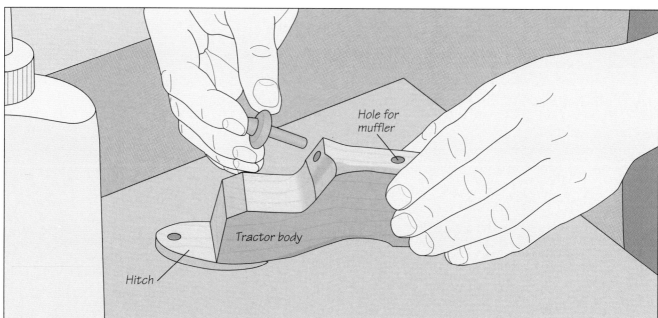

2 Mounting the steering wheel, fuel cap, and muffler
Mark holes on the tractor body for the steering wheel column, fuel cap, and muffler. Bore $^7/_{32}$-inch-diameter holes for the column and cap, and a $^5/_{32}$-inch-diameter hole for the muffler. Make all the holes ¼ inch deep. Fashion the steering wheel by attaching a ¾-inch wheel to a $^7/_{32}$-inch-diameter dowel. Make the fuel cap from a wood button or peg with a short shaft; a length of $^5/_{32}$-inch dowel can form the muffler. Dab glue into the three holes and set each piece in place *(above).* (It is easier to sand the pieces before gluing them in position.) To finish the muffler, drill a $^5/_{32}$-inch-diameter hole through the middle of a $^3/_8$-inch dowel, spread some glue in the hole, and slip the dowel over the smaller peg already in place.

3 Installing the front axle and wheels

Cut the axle on your band saw from a piece of 1-by-2⅜-inch-thick stock and sand its surfaces smooth. You need to drill three 7⁄32-inch-diameter holes into the axle: one in each side for the wheels and a third in the top to attach the axle to the tractor body. Clamp a backup panel to your drill press table and secure the axle in a handscrew as you bore each hole *(right)*. Drill a matching hole into the underside of the tractor. You can make the front wheels on the lathe *(page 33)*, then glue them to the axle and attach the axle to the tractor body using pegs and glue. The peg securing the axle to the body can be left a little long to allow the axle to swivel.

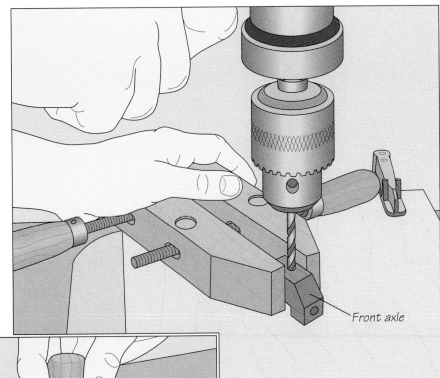

Front axle

Mudguard

Fender base   *Taillight hole*

4 Gluing the fenders

Cut the two parts of each fender assembly on your band saw, making the bases from ¼-inch-thick stock and the mudguards from ½-inch-thick stock. The pieces on opposite sides of the tractor should be mirror images of each other. Drill holes into the ends of the mudguards for the buttons and dowels that will serve as the lights, then glue the mudguards to their respective fender bases. Once the adhesive has cured, glue the fender assemblies to the tractor body, making sure the bottom edges of the pieces are flush with each other. Use a handscrew to hold the fenders in position while the adhesive cures *(left)*. Glue wood buttons to the front of the mudguards for headlights and dowels to the back for taillights.

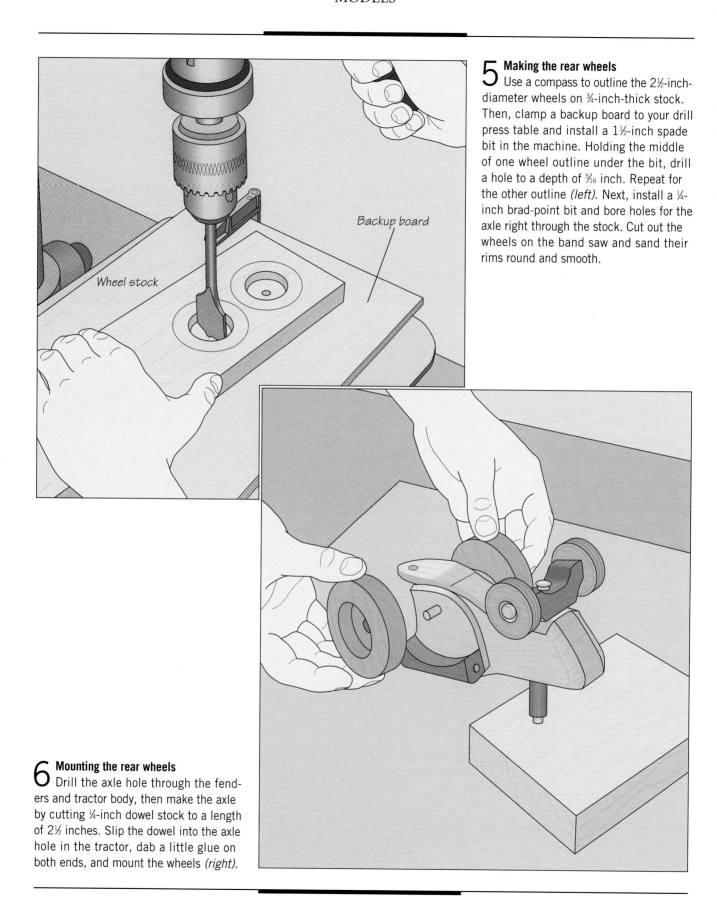

Wheel stock

Backup board

5 Making the rear wheels

Use a compass to outline the 2½-inch-diameter wheels on ¾-inch-thick stock. Then, clamp a backup board to your drill press table and install a 1½-inch spade bit in the machine. Holding the middle of one wheel outline under the bit, drill a hole to a depth of ⁵⁄₁₆ inch. Repeat for the other outline *(left)*. Next, install a ¼-inch brad-point bit and bore holes for the axle right through the stock. Cut out the wheels on the band saw and sand their rims round and smooth.

6 Mounting the rear wheels

Drill the axle hole through the fenders and tractor body, then make the axle by cutting ¼-inch dowel stock to a length of 2½ inches. Slip the dowel into the axle hole in the tractor, dab a little glue on both ends, and mount the wheels *(right)*.

MAKING THE ROCK PICKER

1 Making the fork

Referring to the anatomy illustration on page 37, cut the fork to shape from a piece of ¾-inch-thick stock. Sand all the surfaces, ensuring that the contours are smooth and rounded. Then mark a line across the fork ¾ inch from its thick edge and a series of parallel lines at ³⁄₁₆-inch intervals from the thin edge to the marked line. Make a cut along each of the parallel lines on your band saw *(right)*, feeding the fork with both hands and making sure you keep your fingers clear of the blade.

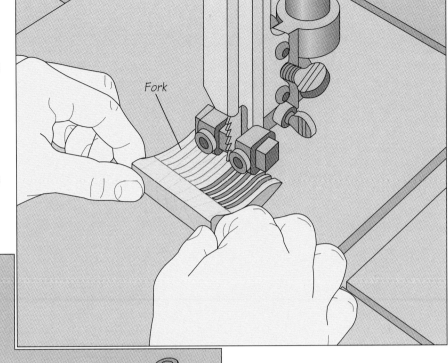

Fork

2 Shaping the reel ends

Make the reel ends by cutting out two 1¼-inch-diameter wheels from ¼-inch-thick stock. Sand the wheels smooth and drill a ⁷⁄₁₆-inch-diameter axle hole through each one. To make the indentations along the edges of the wheels, mark six radius lines spaced 60° apart. You can then cut the indentations by hand with a tapered half-round file or on an oscillating spindle sander with a thin spindle. On a spindle sander, you will need to make a V-block jig to do the job. For the jig, cut a 130° angle wedge out of a board, then drill a hole through the jig centered on the angle's apex; the hole should be large enough to accommodate the spindle. Clamp the jig to the sanding table, centering the spindle in the hole. Turn on the sander, advance the reel flat on the table with both index fingers so that one of the radius lines is aligned with the spindle, and cut the indentation to a depth of ¼ inch *(left)*. Repeat for the remaining indentations.

V-block jig

Reel end

3 Assembling the reel

Install a ⅛-inch bit in your drill press and bore a stopped hole into the middle of each projection on the inside faces of the reel ends. Make each hole ⅛ inch deep. To join the reel ends together, cut a 2³⁄₃₂-inch-long dowel for each pair of holes. Then dab some glue in the holes, insert the dowels into one of the wheels, and fit the second wheel on top *(left)*.

4 Gluing up the body

On your band saw, cut the parts of the rock picker's body, including the sidewalls, the base, and the bucket. Glue the bucket sidewall to the interior. To prepare the sidewalls for assembly, you need to drill four holes in each one: one each for the bucket, wheels, fork, and reel. The holes for the fork and bucket should be ⁵⁄₃₂ inch in diameter; make the holes for the reel and wheels ⁷⁄₃₂ inch in diameter. Once all the holes are drilled, use a dowel and glue to join the bucket to the sidewalls *(right)*. Attach the reel between the sidewalls with wooden pegs and glue the base in place.

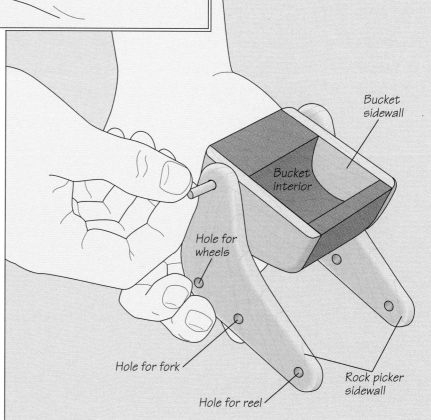

Bucket sidewall

Bucket interior

Hole for wheels

Hole for fork

Hole for reel

Rock picker sidewall

5 Installing the hitch

Cut the hitch to shape on your band saw and sand its surfaces smooth. Drill holes in the hitch for the wheel pegs and the peg that will join the hitch to the tractor. Then spread glue on the contacting surfaces of the hitch and sidewall, and clamp the hitch in place on a work table *(right)*.

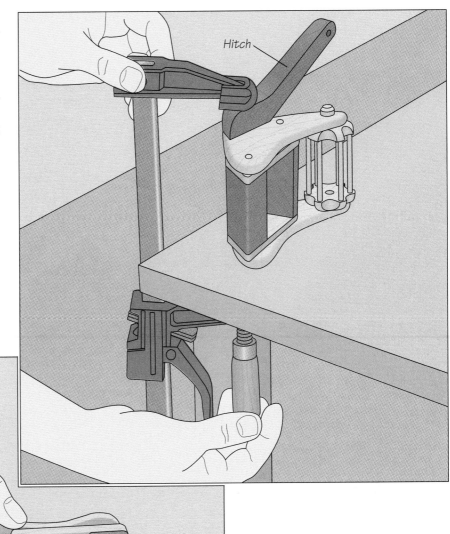

Hitch

6 Mounting the fork and the wheels

Use glue and a dowel to attach the fork to the sidewalls. To complete the project, use glue and wooden pegs to join the wheels to the rock picker *(left)*. You are now ready to apply a finish.

SLEIGHS AND SLEDS

Today, sleighs and sleds conjure up images of children on bright winter afternoons coasting down snow-covered hills, squealing with joy. The origins of the conveyances featured in this chapter, however, are far more practical. In northern regions of the world, the sled evolved centuries ago as a humble yet efficient carrier, transporting food and belongings over ice and snow. From the Inuit dogsled and the Laplander pulka to the Russian troika and the American "one-horse open sleigh," sleds provided the edge that pre-industrial northerners needed to survive on snowy terrain.

Each of the three pieces described in this chapter can trace its lineage to one or more of these early antecedents. The bent-runner sleigh pictured above and at left is a refined version of the traditional sled. Its raised-deck design is based on the sleds of Switzerland and Austria. Despite its delicate appearance, the sound construction techniques shown beginning on page 46 will produce a very sturdy sled.

The Yankee clipper *(page 54)* evolved in Colonial America, and has been a popular fixture of winter frolicking since Revolutionary times. Perhaps its most famous incarnation

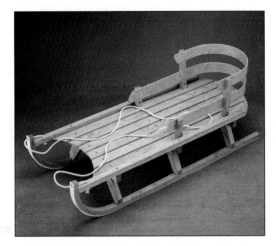

The cherry sleigh shown above is an attractive and sturdy wintertime conveyance for bundled-up infants and toddlers. Once a child outgrows the need to be pulled through the snow, the sleigh can be transformed into a fast-moving sled. The backrest is attached to the seat rails with knock-down connectors. This model is based on a design by Walter Last of Winnipeg, Canada.

was "Rosebud", the sled that played a key symbolic role in Orson Welles' classic 1941 film *Citizen Kane.* You can build yourself a version of this sled with a modest investment in wood.

The toboggan shown on page 58 is not very different from its primitive forerunners, which were used by North American natives long before the arrival of Columbus. Although the toboggan may be based on an ancient design, it is an ingenious means of transportation, perfectly adapted to travel in loose snow, whereas raised-deck sleighs require a packed-snow surface to glide efficiently. The heart of any sled lies in its runners, and each of the three models in this chapter uses a different design. The runners for the low-to-the-ground clipper are the simplest to make. As shown on page 54, they can be cut out on the band saw. The bent-runner sleigh with its raised deck requires stronger runners, which are curved by bending and laminating thin strips of wood. The flat runners for the toboggan—constituting both deck and gliding surface—are flexed to such a tight radius that steam bending is the only practical way to make them.

A strip of ultra-high molecular weight plastic is fastened to the underside of the sleigh runners shown at left. Strong, flexible and easy to install, the strips protect the wood runners and will make the sleigh glide better.

BENT-RUNNER SLEIGH

The bent-runner sleigh featured in this section blends traditional sled design with modern woodworking techniques. As shown in the photo below, the legs are attached to the stretchers with plate joints—a simple and sturdy joinery method. The posts supporting the backrest are secured to the deck with screws and metal cross dowels. Using knockdown fasteners in this application allows the backrest to be removed easily, transforming the sleigh into a flat-deck racer. The undersides of the runners are covered with a layer of ultra-high molecular weight plastic, a high-tech material available from most plastics distributors and some woodworking supply houses. It will enhance the runners' slick-ness and make them glide much better on snow.

As described beginning on page 47, the runners and backrest are made of thin wood strips laminated together and bent during glue up. Since both parts share the same curvature, they can be bent on the same form. Oak and ash both have superior bending qualities, and are the best choices if you want strong and tough runners. But other hardwoods, like maple, birch, and beech, can be used. The sleigh shown in the photo on page 44 is made of cherry, another good choice.

Any sled must be built to withstand abuse as well as the elements. Use only stainless steel fasteners and a highly water-resistant adhesive for glue up. Finish the sleigh with marine varnish. Be sure to finish the bottom of the runners before attaching the plastic strips.

A pair of legs for a bent-runner sleigh are glued to one of the stretchers, while a shop-made jig holds the pieces at the correct angle. Plate joints (page 50) are cut to reinforce the connection. Refer to page 51 for instructions on making the clamping jig.

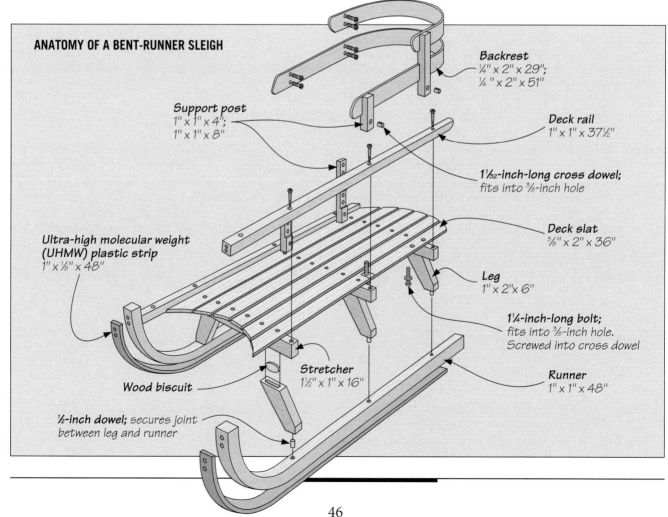

ANATOMY OF A BENT-RUNNER SLEIGH

Backrest
¼" x 2" x 29";
¼" x 2" x 51"

Support post
1" x 1" x 4";
1" x 1" x 8"

Deck rail
1" x 1" x 37½"

1¹⁄₃₂-inch-long cross dowel;
fits into ⅜-inch hole

Deck slat
⅜" x 2" x 36"

**Ultra-high molecular weight
(UHMW) plastic strip**
1" x ⅛" x 48"

Leg
1" x 2" x 6"

1¼-inch-long bolt;
fits into ⅜-inch hole.
Screwed into cross dowel

Wood biscuit

Stretcher
1½" x 1" x 16"

Runner
1" x 1" x 48"

½-inch dowel; secures joint
between leg and runner

MAKING THE RUNNERS

1 Ripping the runner stock
Cut the runner strips on your table saw from a board wide enough to yield all the runners you will need. The board should be slightly thicker than the final width of the runners. Position the rip fence for an ⅛-inch cutting width and feed the workpiece with a push stick *(right)*. Use one hand to press the board flush against the fence, being careful to keep both hands well clear of the blade. Cut an extra strip to use as a clamping caul in step 3.

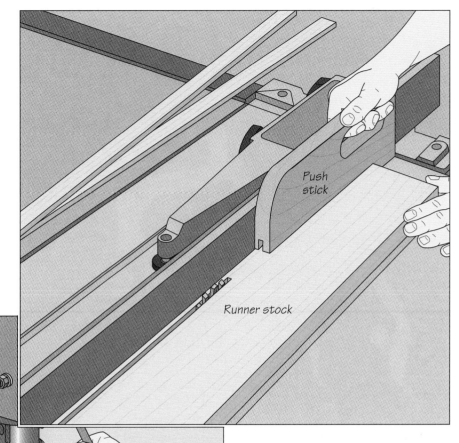

Push stick

Runner stock

2 Making the bending form
To bend both the runner and backrest strips, you will need a shop-made bending form. For the jig, cut three pieces of ¾-inch plywood, mark a circle with a 6-inch radius on their top surfaces, and cut out the curves on your band saw. Also saw a long rectangular slot in the center of each piece. Screw the pieces of the jig together, making sure the ends and edges are aligned. To facilitate clamping the curve, drill a series of holes with a spade bit slightly larger than the clamp jaws you will be using; remember to secure a backup panel to the drill press table to minimize tearout *(left)*.

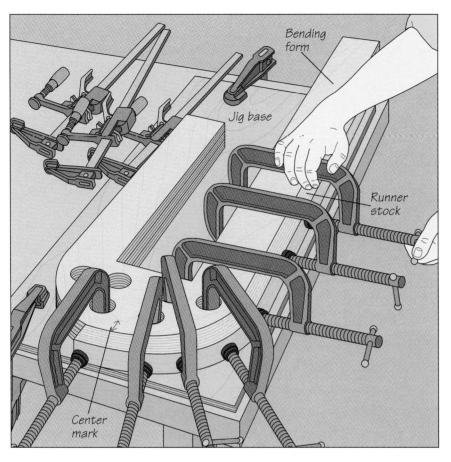

3 Gluing up the runners

Screw the bending form to a base of ¾-inch plywood and clamp the base to a work surface. To prevent the runners from sticking to the form, apply a thin coat of paraffin wax to the form's outside edge. Spread glue on one side of each strip of the runner and stack the pieces, lining up their ends. Leave an extra unglued strip on the outside to protect the strips from the clamp jaws. Place the stack along the outside edge of the form and use clamps to secure the strips against it, starting at the curved end and working to the opposite end *(left)*. Let the setup cure for 8 to 10 hours. Bend the backrest the same way, but align the center of the lamination with the center mark on the form.

4 Jointing the lamination

Once the lamination is dry, remove it from the form and joint one edge. Slowly feed the workpiece across the cutters, using push blocks to feed the workpiece and apply downward pressure on the outside side of the knives *(right)*. Never position your hands directly over the cutters. Next, cut the lamination to its finished thickness on a planer.

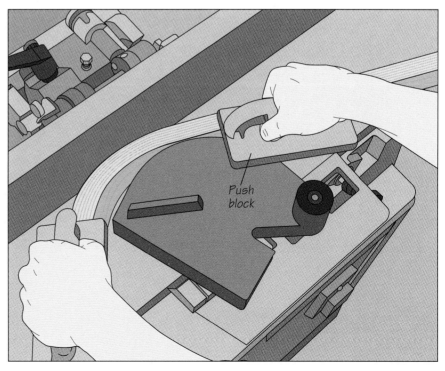

MAKING THE DECK

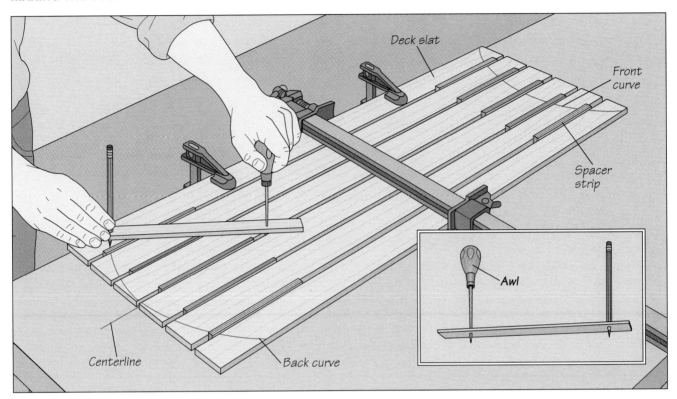

Deck slat

Front curve

Spacer strip

Awl

Centerline

Back curve

1 Preparing the slats

The sleigh's deck has an inward curve at the front end and a matching outward curve at the back. Start by cutting the slats slightly longer than their final length and mark a centerline on a work surface. Then arrange the slats on the table. Place ¼-inch-thick spacer strips between the slats to maintain the proper spacing. Then clamp the slats together edge to edge and secure the assembly to the table, aligning the middle of the deck with the centerline on the table. Next, use a shop-made compass to mark the curves on the slats. For the compass, drill two holes 9 inches apart through a wood strip; one hole should accommodate an awl and the other a pencil (inset). Mark the front curve on the slats so the arc ends about ½ inch from the edges of the outside slats. Draw the back curve so the center of the arc is 36 inches from the center of the front curve (above).

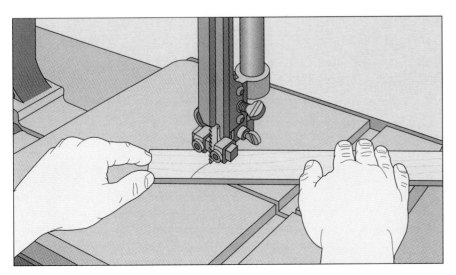

2 Cutting the deck slats

Cut the deck slat curves on a band saw (left), then sand any marks left by the blade; a spindle sander works well for this type of work. Finally, bevel the edges of the slats slightly with a sanding block.

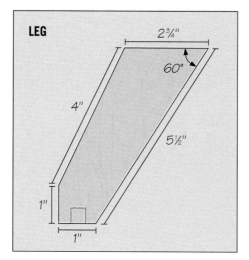

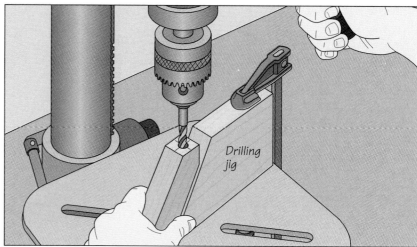

3 Making the legs

Cut your leg blanks from 1-inch-thick stock to a width of 1⅞ inches. Then miter the ends of each blank on your table saw with the miter gauge adjusted to 60°. Next, use a band saw to cut one of the legs to the profile shown *(above, left)*; the finished leg can then serve as a template for cutting the remaining ones. Sand away any marks left by the band saw blade. The legs are joined to the runners with ½-inch-diameter, 1⅛-inch-long dowels. To bore the dowel holes in the legs, mark lines that intersect at the center of their bottom ends. Then miter the end of a board at 60° to create a jig that will brace the workpiece on your drill press table. Install a ½-inch bit in the machine and set the drilling depth to slightly more than one-half the dowel length. Align the center of the leg's bottom end under the bit, clamp the jig alongside the leg and, holding the leg firmly against the table and jig, bore the hole *(above, right)*.

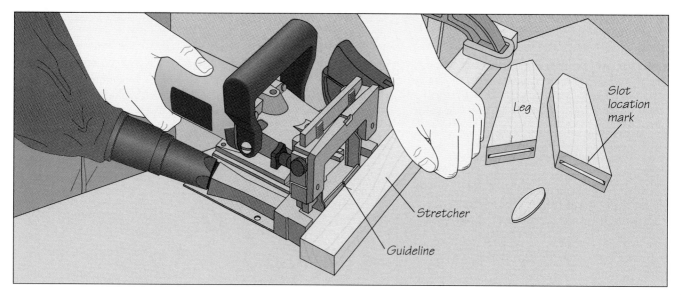

4 Joining the legs to the stretchers

Attach the legs to the stretchers with plate joints—thin, football-shaped biscuits of compressed wood that fit into mating slots. Use the clamping jig shown on page 51 to align the parts and mark center lines for the biscuit slots across the joints between the legs and stretcher. Use a plate joiner to cut a slot into the top end of the legs; hold the workpiece in place with a clamp. Then secure the stretcher to a work surface, align the guideline on the tool's faceplate with the slot location mark on the workpiece, and cut the slot *(above)*. Repeat the procedure at the other slot locations, then glue each pair of legs to its stretcher, as shown in the photo on page 46.

BUILT IT YOURSELF

LEG-CLAMPING JIG

The jig shown at right, made entirely from ¾-inch plywood, makes it easy to align the legs and stretchers of a bent-runner sleigh for marking plate joint slots and gluing up. Cut the pieces so the distance between the inside edges of the leg supports is the same as the length of the sleigh's stretcher. Trim the corners of the stretcher support as shown to accommodate the clamp jaws during glue-up, then screw the strips to the base, making sure that the leg supports are square to the stretcher support. Wax the top surface of the jig to prevent the glued-up assembly (shown in dotted lines) from bonding to it. The photo on page 46 shows the jig in use.

Stretcher
support

Base

Leg support

ASSEMBLING THE SLEIGH

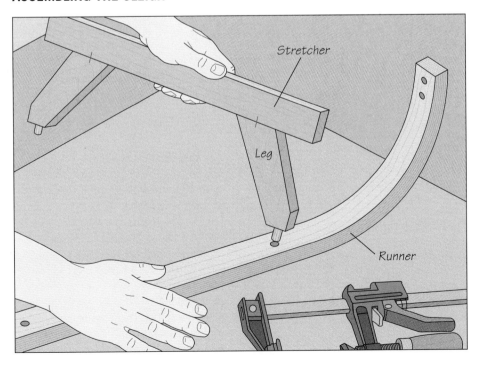

Stretcher

Leg

Runner

1 Attaching the legs to the runners

Position the legs on the runners, then mark the dowel holes on the runners. Bore a hole at each mark slightly deeper than one half the dowel length. Then apply glue in the holes and on the contacting surfaces between the legs and runners, insert a dowel into each hole in the legs, and fit the pieces together *(left)*. Clamp the assembly, making sure the stretchers are perpendicular to the runners.

2 Installing the deck rails

Cut the deck rails to size, curving the back end using the same techniques described on page 49 for the slats. Position the rails on the strechers and against the runners, and apply glue on the contacting surfaces. Clamp the rails in place and drill two pilot holes through the runners into the front end of the rails. Also bore holes through the rails into the stretchers. Attach the rails to the runners and stretchers with counter-sunk stainless steel wood screws *(right)*, removing the clamps as you go.

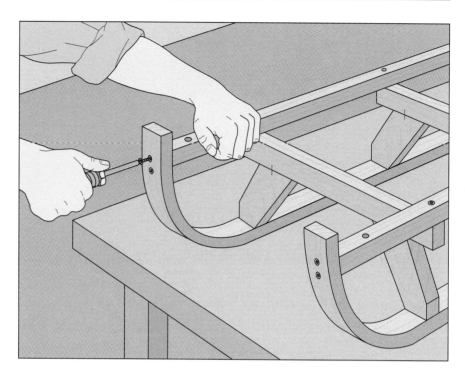

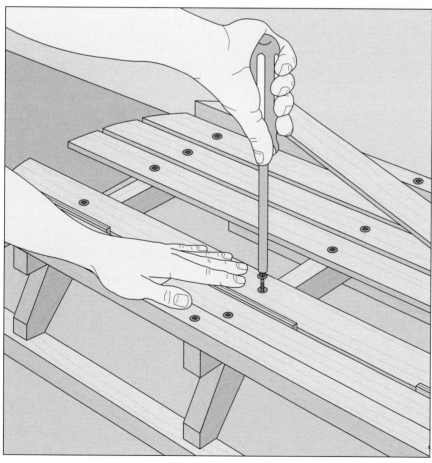

3 Attaching the deck slats

Lay out the slats on the stretchers, spacing them with ¼-inch-thick wood strips. The two center boards should over-hang the front stretcher by about ⅞ inch. Position the other boards so their ends form a smooth curve. Drill countersunk pilot holes through the slats into the stretchers, temporarily remove the slats, and apply a bead of water-resistant glue along the stretchers. Reposition the slats on the stretchers and fasten them in place with stainless steel screws *(left)*.

INSTALLING THE BACKREST

1 Making the support posts
Cut the support posts to size, then mark the notches that will accommodate the backrest, referring to the anatomy illustration on page 46. Cut the notches on your table saw, installing a dado head on the machine. Adjust the cutting height to the thickness of the backrest slats, then screw a board to the miter gauge as an extension. Holding the workpiece flush against the extension, align the end of the notch outline with the blades, butt a wood block against the workpiece, and clamp it to the extension as a stop block. Holding the stock against the extension and the stop block, feed the workpiece into the dado head. Keep both hands clear of the blades. Make a series of passes to finish cutting the notch, shifting the workpiece sideways as necessary. For the back post shown, turn the stock around and repeat to cut the second notch *(right)*. Cut the notch on the front post the same way. Once all the notches are cut, screw the backrest to the posts.

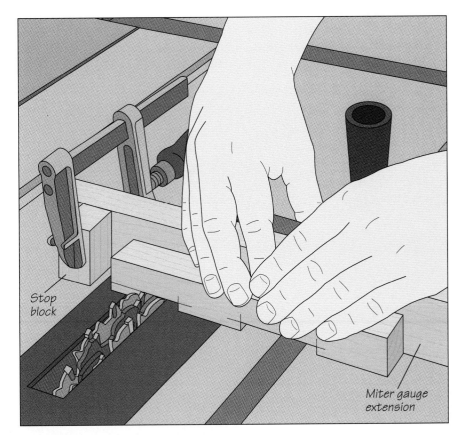

Stop block

Miter gauge extension

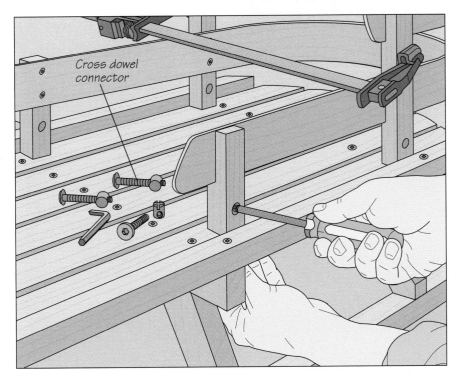

Cross dowel connector

2 Attaching the backrest to the sleigh
The backrest is secured to the sled with $^{11}\!/_{32}$-inch metal cross dowel connectors. To prepare the support posts, drill a 1¼-inch-long ⅜-inch-diameter hole into the end of each one. Also bore a ⅜-inch-diameter hole through the center of each post 1 inch from the bottom. Drill another set of holes through the deck slats at each post location to accommodate the bolts. Fit a cross dowel into each hole in the posts, then position the backrest on the sleigh. Install a clamp across the back support posts to bend the backrest to the correct width, install the bolts up through the deck and into the posts, and tighten them by hand. Use a screwdriver to align the cross dowel *(left)*, then finish tightening the bolts from underneath with a hex wrench.

YANKEE CLIPPER

The design of the clipper shown in this section evolved as a response to the abuse dished out by New England winters—and the young owners of these sleds. It is made from carefully chosen wood, held together by a simple, rugged method of construction. The Yankee Clipper consists of only five main parts: two runners, two stretchers, and a deck. The stretchers are joined to the runners with round mortise-and-tenon joints, which are then pegged with hardwood dowels. Use a tough wood like ash or oak for the runners and stretchers.

To keep the weight of the sled to a minimum, make the deck from a light species, such as white pine. For maximum strength, glue the deck to the stretchers. Although this approach does not allow for expansion or contraction of the deck, you can compensate by selecting wood that is free from checks and reinforcing the connection with screws.

The secret to a fast sled lies in the runners. In the 18th and 19th Centuries, the best sleds had shoes of silver steel polished to a mirror finish. Today, mild steel is a reasonable substitute. You can buy ¹⁄₁₆-by-¾ inch bars at most hardware stores and burnish the finished runners with a belt sander.

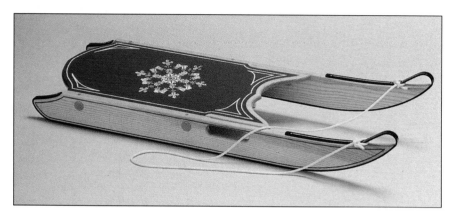

The snowflake design on the clipper shown above transforms a simple plaything into an attractive and elegant sled. As shown on page 56, such designs can be stenciled onto the deck with a thick-bodied paint, such as quick-drying japan colors or acrylic paint. This sled was built by John Sollinger of North Ferrisburg, Vermont.

MAKING THE FRAME

1 Making the runners

Outline the runners on a piece of ¼-inch plywood or hardboard and cut it out as a template on your band saw. Use a compass to outline the mortises for the stretcher tenons on the template. They should be positioned so that when the seat deck is installed *(page 56)*, its surface will be flush with the top of the runners. Drill a ⅛-inch hole at the mark left by the compass point. (This will serve to center the spade bit that you will use later to drill the mortise.) Outline the handle, then cut it out with a scroll saw or coping saw, then trace the design onto your runner stock *(right)*, marking points for the mortises. Cut the runners using a band saw and the handle with a scroll saw or coping saw, then bore the mortises on a drill press fitted with a 1-inch spade bit. Sand all the edges of the runners.

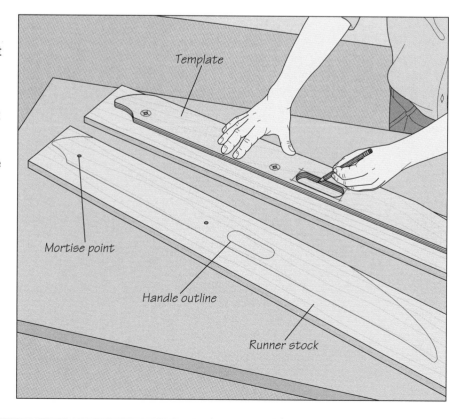

Template

Mortise point

Handle outline

Runner stock

2 Turning the stretchers

Make the stretchers from 1⅛-inch-square stock, cut about ½ inch longer than you need. Mount the blank between centers on your lathe and use a parting tool to turn a 1-inch-diameter tenon on each end. Use calipers to check the tenon diameter as you go *(right)*. Trim the ends of the tenons, if necessary, but they should be long enough to pass completely through the runners.

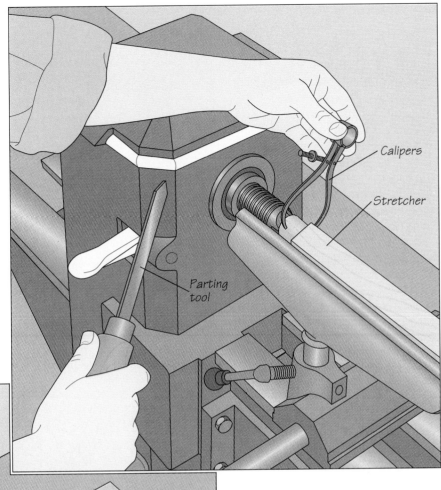

Calipers

Stretcher

Parting
tool

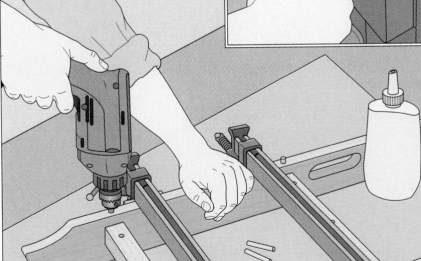

Wood pad

3 Assembling the frame

Spread glue on the tenons on the stretchers and in the runner mortises and fit the pieces together, using a mallet to tap the joints together, if necessary. Rotate the stretchers so that their top surfaces are parallel to the top edges of the runners, then secure the assembly with two bar clamps, protecting the stock with wood pads and aligning the clamps with the strechers. Next, reinforce the joints with dowels. Holding the frame steady on a work surface, drill a hole for a ¼-inch dowel into the top edge of each runner and through each stretcher tenon *(left)*. After boring each hole, dab a little glue into it and tap in a dowel. Once all the dowels are installed, trim them flush with a chisel.

FINISHING THE DECK

1 Securing the seat
Make the seat by edge-gluing boards together *(page 98)*, then plane it to a thickness of ⁹⁄₁₆ inch. Cut the seat to fit snugly between the runners then, referring to the color photo on page 54, cut the ends of the seat to shape on your band saw, round over the edges, and sand them smooth. With the seat upside down on a work surface, spread glue on the tops of the stretchers and clamp the seat to the frame, using wood pads to protect the stock. For added strength, drill a series of countersunk pilot holes through the stretchers and into the seat. To avoid boring through the seat, mark the drilling depth—the thickness of the stretchers plus no more than one-half the thickness of the seat—on the drill bit with a piece of masking tape. Drive a stainless steel wood screw into each hole *(right)*.

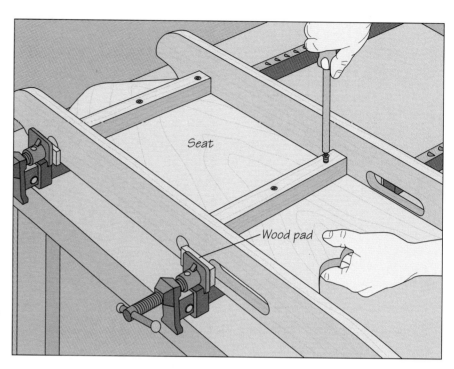

Seat

Wood pad

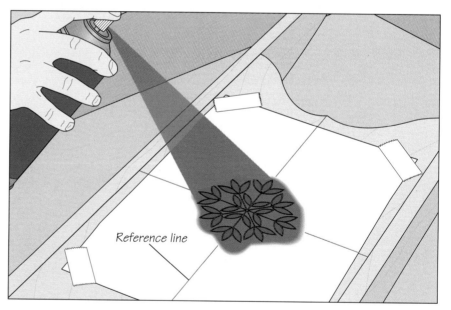

Reference line

2 Making a stencil
Make a photocopy of the stencil design, enlarging or reducing the image, as appropriate. Then use carbon paper to transfer the design to a piece of stencil board. Cut out the pattern with a craft knife, pulling the knife toward you *(above)*. (A snowflake pattern is shown on the back endsheet.)

3 Painting the seat
To help align the stencil precisely, draw reference lines centered on both the seat and the stencil. Then align the reference lines and secure the stencil to the seat with masking tape. If you are spraying the paint, hold an aerosol paint can 6 to 10 inches from the surface and direct the spray at the stencil until the exposed wood is coated lightly with paint *(above)*. You can also use a stenciling brush to apply the paint. To avoid any bleeding, remove the stencil while the paint is wet. Finish the sled with several coats of marine varnish.

FASTENING STEEL SHOES TO THE RUNNERS

1 Bending the shoes
Make a third sleigh runner *(page 54)* to use as a bending form for the steel shoes. As shown in the color photo on page 54, this runner will need a bulge along the top at the front end to form a loop that with anchor the tow rope. Measure along the edge of the runner, cut the steel to length using a hacksaw, and file off any burrs. Mark screw holes on the shoes at every transition point along the runner's edge, then drill a countersunk hole through the shoe at each point. To bend the shoe around the runner, start at the back end; you may need the help of a machinist's vise. Hold the shoe in place with a C clamp, then repeat the process at the front end of the runner *(right)*.

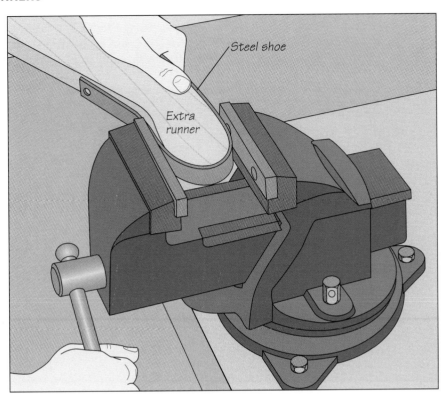

Steel shoe

Extra runner

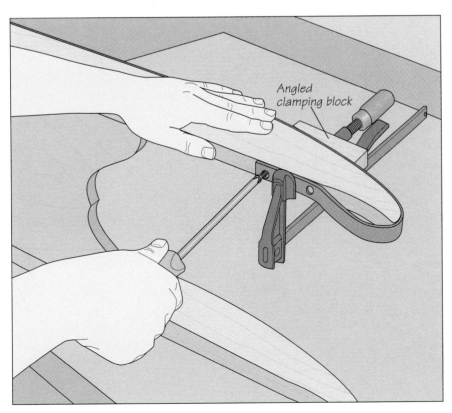

Angled clamping block

2 Securing the shoes
Set the sleigh on its side on a work surface, then start installing a shoe at the front end of one of the runners. Holding or clamping the shoe tight against the runner, drill a pilot hole into the runner, using the hole in the shoe as a guide. You may need to cut an angled clamping block to keep the clamp jaws square to the shoe. Then drive a screw in place *(left)*. Repeat the process at the next hole and continue until both shoes are installed. Because the steel will tend to creep forward as each screw is tightened, drill each pilot hole only after the previous screw has been driven.

TOBOGGAN

The flat-bottomed toboggan is a means of transportation perfectly adapted to its environment. The runners are made by steam bending narrow slats around a form. They are then fastened to crosspieces. A rope is threaded through the crosspieces and serves two purposes: setting and holding the nose curve and providing a hand-hold for breathtaking downhill rides.

Since the runners also serve as this sled's deck and seat, it is important to bend them precisely. They should have a radius of 3½ to 4 inches, with the curl tightening slightly toward the end. For best results, use a wood with superior bending qualities such as maple or ash planed to ⅜ inch thick.

To finish a toboggan, seal the top surface with a coat of marine varnish. The bottom should be treated with hot pine tar, available from ski shops. This will seal the wood and provide a surface to hold the runner wax. Work in the pine tar with a rag, using a propane torch on a very low heat setting to keep the tar fluid. To prepare the toboggan for a day on the hills, rub on a layer of hard cross-country ski glide wax with a cork block.

The toboggan shown at left was made from steam-bent maple. Also known as a Canadian sled, this version is long and sturdy enough to carry two or three riders over the deepest snow.

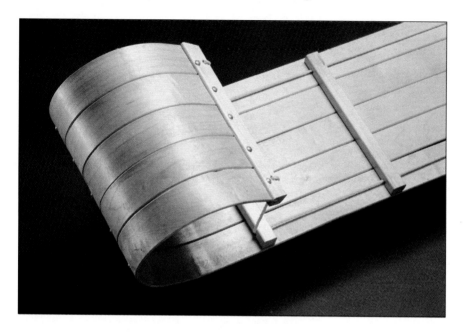

MAKING THE RUNNERS

1 Preparing the slats

Toboggans generally range in size from 3-foot single-seaters up to 6-foot models for two or three riders. Once you have chosen a length, make your slats 16 inches longer to form the bend at the nose. Cut the slats 2¼ inches wide from ⅜-inch-thick stock. Next, smooth the edges of each slat on a table-mounted router. Fit the tool with a ⅛-inch piloted round-over bit and use three featherboards to help you guide the slats across the table. Clamp one to the table in line with the bit and brace it with a support board, and fix the other two to the fence on either side of the cutter. (In the illustration, the featherboard on the outfeed side of the bit has been removed for clarity.) Feed the slats with both hands *(right)*.

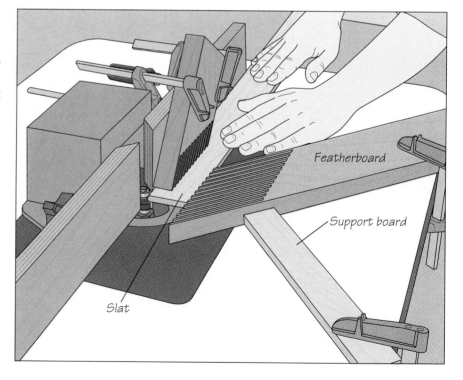

Featherboard

Support board

Slat

2 Steaming the slats

Build a steamer like the one shown at right from two lengths of Schedule 80 ABS pipe joined by an ABS T connector. Use push-on end caps to prevent the steamer from becoming over-pressurized. Glue a ½-inch connector pipe to the T connector and attach the connector to a commercial wallpaper steamer. To hold the wood above condensed water in the pipes, install a series of ⅜-inch zinc-coated machine bolts just below the centerline of the pipes. Use both steel and rubber washers to make an airtight seal. Also drill a ½-inch drain hole at one end. Lastly, build a 2-by-4 frame that will support the steamer on a slight incline to allow condensed water to run out of the drain hole. To use the steamer, secure the push-on caps, turn on the device, and let the steamer warm up. Once steam begins to escape from the drain hole, place a slat inside. Close the end cap tightly and let the wood steam for about 30 minutes. To avoid scalding your hands, wear work gloves and use tongs when removing the wood from the steamer *(inset)*.

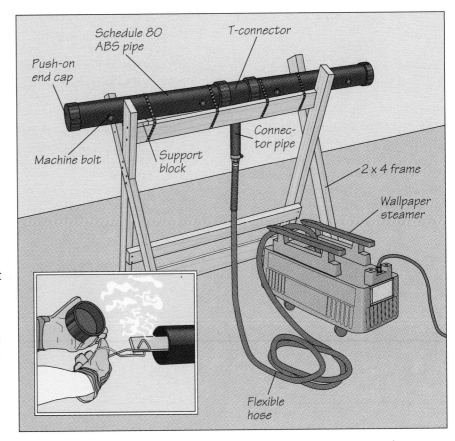

3 Bending the slats

Cut a bending form from a board as thick as the width of the slats, following the profile of the toboggan. Screw the form to a base made from two ¾-inch plywood sheets and clamp the base to a work surface. Bore three 1-inch-diameter holes through the base for locking dowels around the curved part of the form. The space between the dowels and the edge of the form should equal the slat thickness. When you remove a slat from the steamer, place it on the form and use a wedge to secure the front end. Working quickly, bend the slat firmly and steadily, inserting dowels to secure the workpiece as you proceed *(left)*. Use bar clamps to secure the slat to the straight edge of the form. Leave the slats on the form until they are cool to the touch—about 1 hour. The slats may spring back 1 or 2 inches, but the correct curve will be maintained with the rope.

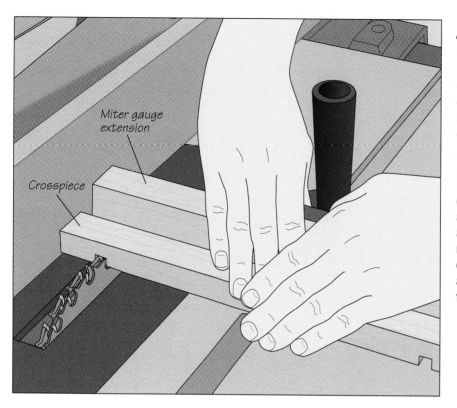

Miter gauge extension

Crosspiece

4 Making the crosspieces
Make the crosspieces from 1-inch-thick, ¾-inch-wide stock and cut the pieces slightly shorter than the combined width of the slats. To cut the notches in the crosspieces for the tow rope, install a dado head in your table saw, adjusting its width and the cutting height to ⅜ inch. Screw a board as an extension to the miter gauge and position the rip fence to make the cut 1 inch from the end of the crosspiece. Holding the workpiece flush against the extension and the fence, cut a notch, then turn the board around and repeat to cut the notch near the other end *(left)*. You will need one crosspiece at each end of the toboggan and at 11- to 13-inch intervals between.

5 Attaching the crosspieces to the slat
Arrange the slats on a work surface, align their ends, and butt their edges together. Spread glue on the underside of a crosspiece and clamp it across the slats about 2 inches from the back end; make sure the crosspiece is perpendicular to the edges of the slats. Glue another crosspiece in the middle of the bend at the front end. Install the remaining pieces at uniform intervals in between. Then turn the toboggan over and drill countersunk pilot holes through each slat at every crosspiece location; bore two holes through the outside slats and one hole through the others. Mark the drilling depth on the drill bit to avoid boring through the crosspieces. Then drive a screw into each hole *(right)*.

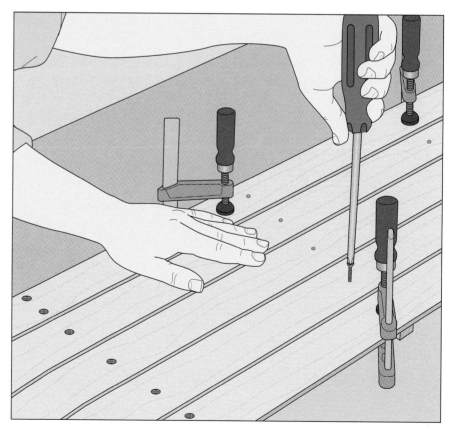

6 Preparing the crown piece

Make the crown piece that will cover the front ends of the slats from the same stock you used for the crosspieces, but cut it about twice as wide and slightly longer. With the same dado head adjustment you used in step 4, raise the cutting height to ¾ inch. Center an edge of the workpiece over the dado head and butt the rip fence against the stock. Also clamp a braced featherboard to the table in line with the blades. Then use a push stick to feed the piece into the dado head, cutting a groove along the bottom edge *(right)*. Fit the piece over the ends of the slats, then drill pilot holes through it at each slat location. Secure the piece in place with stainless steel screws. Also bore a hole through the crown piece near each end for the tow rope. Use a belt sander to smooth the edges of the outside slats flush with the ends of the crown piece, and bevel the edges of the cross pieces with a sanding block, eliminating any sharp edges.

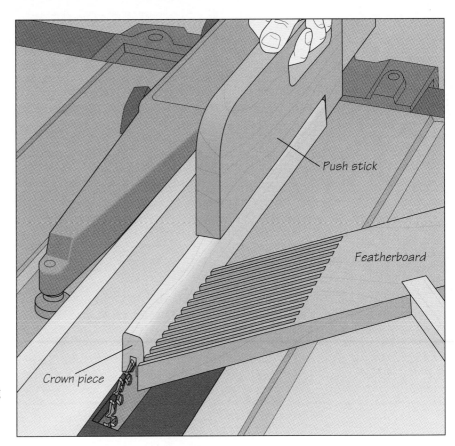

Push stick

Featherboard

Crown piece

7 Finishing the toboggan

Finish the top surface of the toboggan with a coat of marine varnish and the bottom with pine tar *(page 58)*. The final touch is installing the tow rope. With the toboggan flat on a work surface, use a pair of clamps to hold the nose at the desired bend. Then knot one end of the rope and thread it through one hole in the crown piece and through the notches in all the crosspieces. Feed the rope across the back-end crosspiece, then back up through the remaining notches and knot at the front *(left)*. After releasing the clamps, make sure the pressure is equal on both sides of the toboggan. Adjust the knots, if necessary. The toboggan nose should have a fair amount of spring without overstressing the wood.

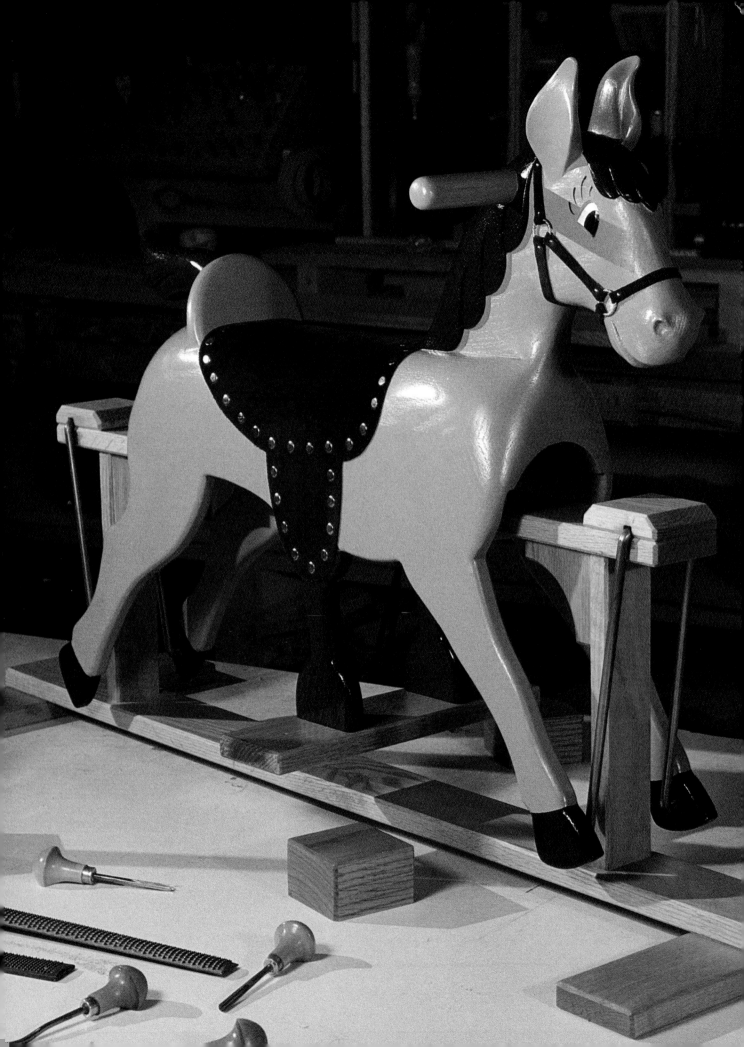

ROCKING HORSES

The modern rocking horse, made mobile by curved wood runners or springs, has been a fixture of childhood for most of the 20th Century. The swing and sway of riding an animal undoubtedly has primordial appeal, dating to the time when animals were first domesticated by humans.

This chapter presents detailed instructions for building three different, but equally delightful, rocking horses. The first version, shown in the photo at left and beginning on page 64, comes closest to duplicating the shape, coloring, and appearance of a horse. This horse is attached to a sturdy stand by means of metal rods fixed to the animal's hooves. The rods enable the horse to swing pendulum-like without any danger of the toy falling over. Among the most useful features of this horse are the footrests positioned outside the stirrups. By fastening wood blocks to the rests, you can fit the horse to the size of the child using it.

Despite its elegance and realistic appearance, the horse is relatively easy to assemble from either solid wood or plywood. Carving the lifelike details of the head and tail, and the shaping of the body will provide an opportunity to expand—or display—your woodworking skills.

As a way of personalizing a rocking horse, you can design one with interchangeable heads. The deer head shown above, carved by Fred Sneath of Stony Lake, Ontario, has a mortise that fits over a tenon in the framework of his swinging horse, featured on page 78. Glued into the head, the antlers come from a living deer, dropped by a male after its rutting season.

The swinging horse shown beginning on page 78 relies on a more stylized rendering of the equine form, but it has several ingenious features. First, it is easy and inexpensive to build from 2-by-4 stock. Second, some of the parts pivot, enabling the horse to be folded and stored. Third, the horse has two seats, a small one for a young child and a larger one behind for an older child or adult. Finally, as shown in the photo at left, the head fits onto the framework with a glueless mortise-and-tenon, allowing different heads to be used.

The final project, featured starting on page 82, is a more traditional rocking horse for a toddler. Easy to build, this horse sits on bent-laminated runners and has a saddle seat supported by a cross beam. This horse stands close to the ground, making it ideal for the small child who is not quite ready for a swinging or stand-mounted animal.

Part of the allure of a rocking horse is a lifelike finish. Refer to the Toy and Crafts Basics chapter starting on page 12 for information on choosing and applying child-safe paints and finishing products. To protect the young users of these horses, round over all contours and edges, sand all surfaces smooth, and avoid any sharp corners or pinch points.

The stand-mounted horse shown at left, built by Don Buhler of Swan River, Manitoba, is designed to adapt to its rider's growth spurts. For a child whose legs do not reach the footrests, wood blocks can be fastened to the rests. As the child grows, smaller blocks can be used or removed altogether. The horse features a hand-carved head and tail, a leather halter, and a suede saddle.

STAND-MOUNTED ROCKING HORSE

ANATOMY OF A STAND-MOUNTED ROCKING HORSE

The rocking horse shown below measures 23 inches high by 33 inches long. It can be fashioned from virtually any stock, although a wood suitable for carving (pine or basswood, for example) should be used for any of the parts that need shaping, such as the head and tail. The legs and body can be constructed of plywood, which will save you the concern of making sure that the grain follows the length of pieces for maximum strength. However, you will have to cover the plies with edge banding.

SIDE VIEW

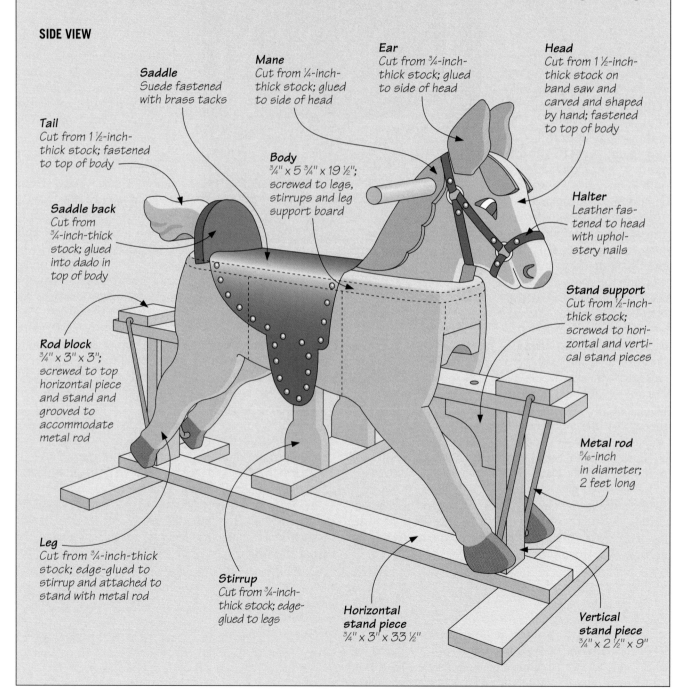

Saddle
Suede fastened with brass tacks

Mane
Cut from ¼-inch-thick stock; glued to side of head

Ear
Cut from ¾-inch-thick stock; glued to side of head

Head
Cut from 1½-inch-thick stock on band saw and carved and shaped by hand; fastened to top of body

Tail
Cut from 1½-inch-thick stock; fastened to top of body

Body
¾" x 5¾" x 19½"; screwed to legs, stirrups and leg support board

Halter
Leather fastened to head with upholstery nails

Saddle back
Cut from ¾-inch-thick stock; glued into dado in top of body

Stand support
Cut from ½-inch-thick stock; screwed to horizontal and vertical stand pieces

Rod block
¾" x 3" x 3"; screwed to top horizontal piece and stand and grooved to accommodate metal rod

Metal rod
⁵⁄₁₆-inch in diameter; 2 feet long

Leg
Cut from ¾-inch-thick stock; edge-glued to stirrup and attached to stand with metal rod

Stirrup
Cut from ¾-inch-thick stock; edge-glued to legs

Horizontal stand piece
¾" x 3" x 33½"

Vertical stand piece
¾" x 2½" x 9"

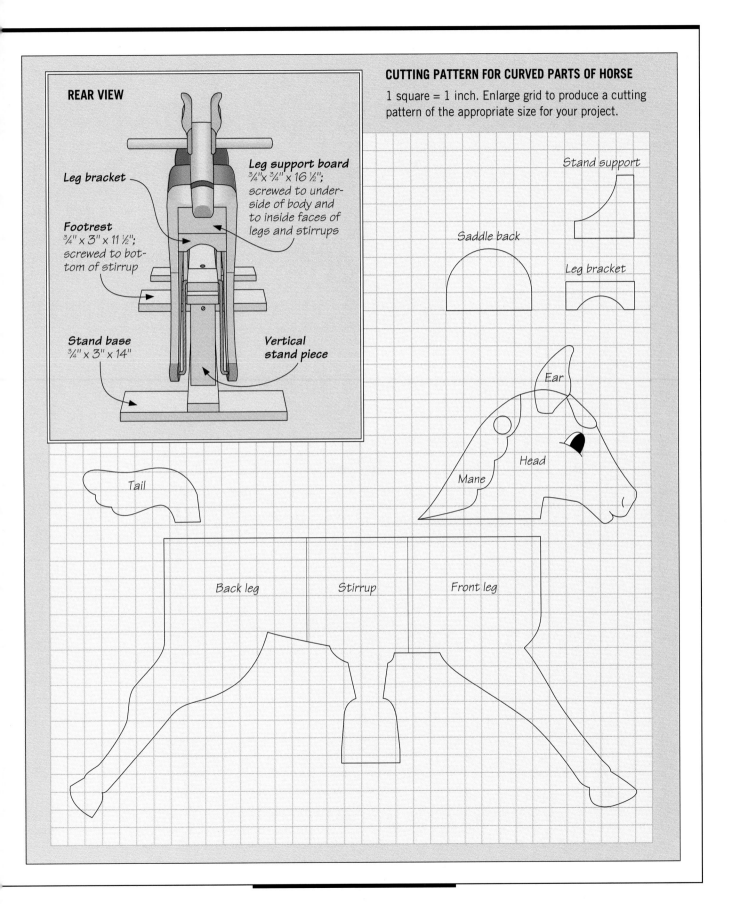

REAR VIEW

Leg bracket

Footrest
¾" x 3" x 11 ½";
screwed to bottom of stirrup

Leg support board
¾" x ¾" x 16 ½";
screwed to underside of body and
to inside faces of
legs and stirrups

Stand base
¾" x 3" x 14"

Vertical
stand piece

CUTTING PATTERN FOR CURVED PARTS OF HORSE

1 square = 1 inch. Enlarge grid to produce a cutting
pattern of the appropriate size for your project.

Stand support

Saddle back

Leg bracket

Ear

Mane

Head

Tail

Back leg

Stirrup

Front leg

The saddle back for a rocking horse is cut out on the band saw from a piece of ¾-inch-thick stock. Once it is sanded smooth, the saddle back will be glued into an angled dado in the body of the horse. Most of the horse's parts, including the legs, body and head, are cut out on the band saw.

PREPARING THE STOCK

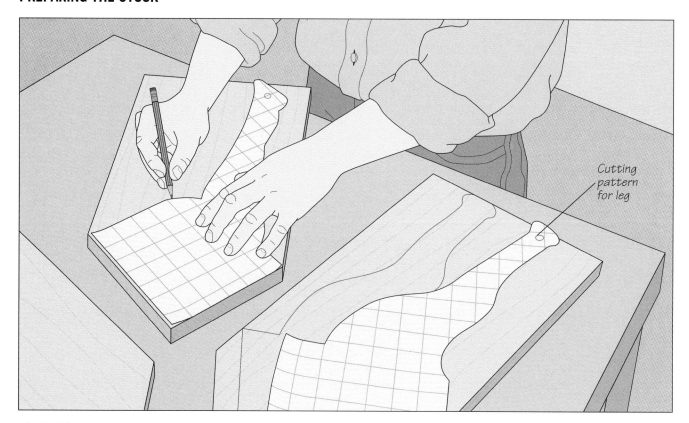

Cutting pattern for leg

1 Outlining the cutting pattern on the stock
Prepare blanks for the parts of the horse that will be produced from your cutting pattern *(page 65)*. These include the legs, stirrups, head, ears, tail, and saddle back. Using ¾-inch plywood or, as shown above, solid wood, make the blanks slightly larger than the pattern. For greatest strength, ensure that the wood grain follows the length of pieces like the legs and stirrups. Holding the appropriate piece of the pattern on each blank in turn, trace its outline on the stock with a pencil *(above)*.

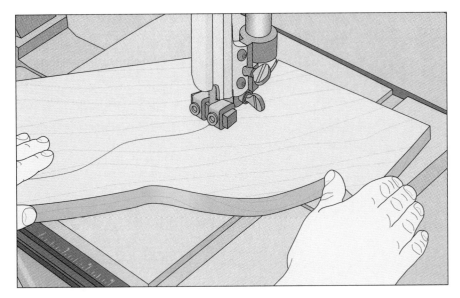

2 Sawing parts to size

Once the parts for one side of the horse have been outlined, cut them to size on your band saw. Cut just to the waste side of your cutting line *(left)*, feeding the stock with both hands and keeping your fingers clear of the blade. Once the parts for one side of the horse are sawn and sanded to the line, use them as patterns to outline the pieces for the other side.

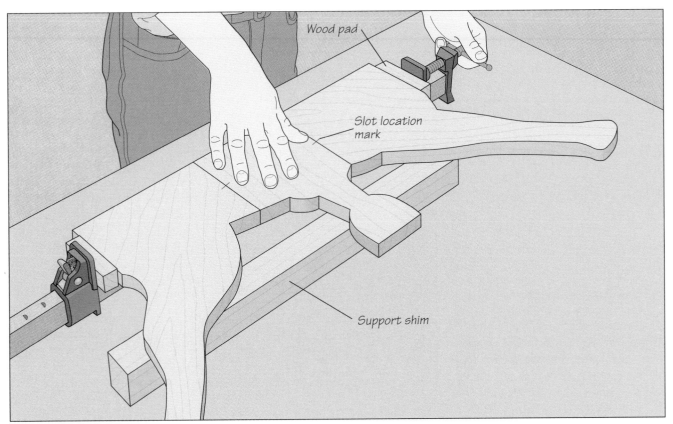

Wood pad

Slot location mark

Support shim

3 Gluing up the legs and stirrups

Dry-fit the legs and stirrup for one side of the horse together and mark a line for a biscuit, or plate, joint across the center of each seam. Use a plate joiner to cut a slot into the mating edges of the pieces at each mark. Then spread glue along the edges and into the slots, insert a wood biscuit into each slot in the legs, and press the pieces together. Protecting the stock with wood pads, secure the joints with a bar clamp *(above)*. Position the clamp jaws at the square ends of the legs and set the bottom end of the assembly on a support shim to hold the pieces level while the glue cures. Repeat the process for the other side of the horse.

SHAPING THE EARS, HEAD, AND TAIL

The ears of a rocking horse can be smoothed to their final shape most easily on a spindle sander. Although you can use a rasp for shaping, the sander removes waste wood more efficiently and is also ideal for smoothing marks left by the band saw blade. Spindles of various sizes can be installed to suit the curve of the piece being shaped. The spindle moves up and down while it rotates, preventing the paper from clogging and allowing you to use the full surface of the sanding drum. After power sanding the parts, use progressively finer grits of sandpaper to hand-sand all surfaces.

1 Carving the eyes and nostrils
Cut the horse's head to shape so the wood grain is oriented across the piece, then outline the eyes and nostrils on each side. Refer to the anatomy illustration on page 64 for the placement and size of these details. Then clamp the head to a work surface and use a carving gouge of the appropriate size to form the eyes and nostrils. Holding the tool vertically with the blade on your outline, strike the handle with a wooden mallet to cut about ¼ inch deep into the wood. Make a second cut *(right)*, then clean up the cavity with a chisel. Repeat the process to carve the nostril.

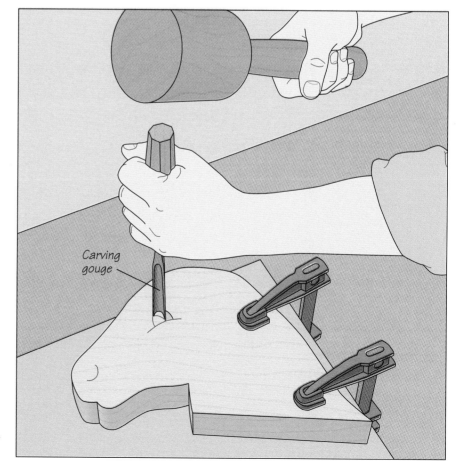

Carving gouge

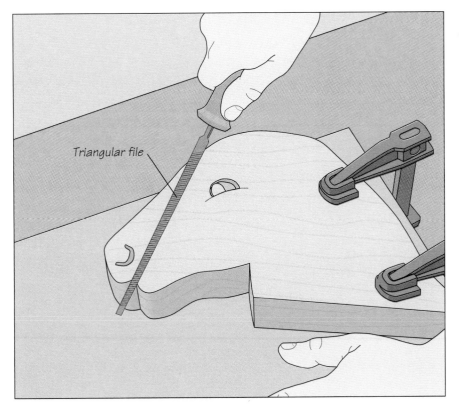

Triangular file

2 Shaping the mouth

Once the eye and nostril are done, use a triangular file to clean up the mouth opening *(left)*. Then turn the workpiece, reclamp it and repeat the process of carving the eyes and nostrils and shaping the mouth on the other side. Use the file in the same way to shape and add detail to the tail.

3 Shaping the head

Once all the surface details have been carved into the head, secure the piece vertically in a bench vise and use a rasp to round over its edges *(below)*. Leave the bottom end of the head flat, however, to facilitate joining it to the body.

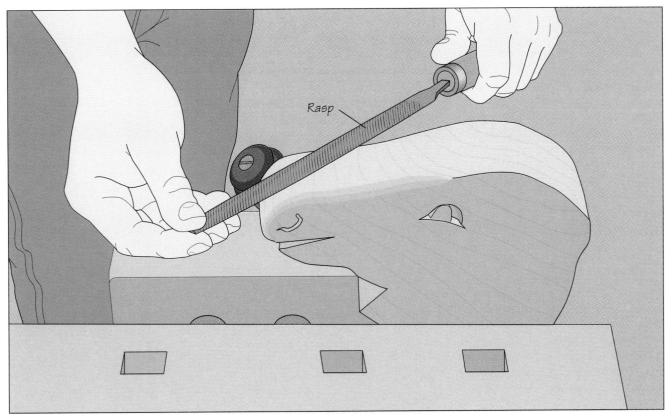

Rasp

ASSEMBLING THE HEAD AND THE BODY

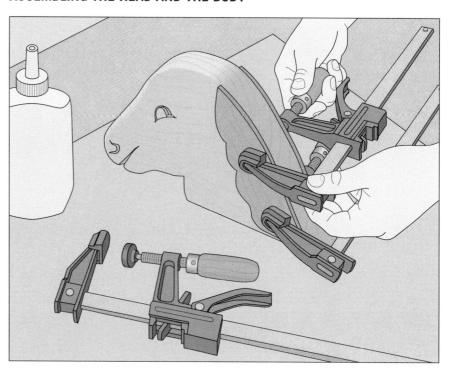

Most of the joinery for assembling a stand-mounted rocking horse is simple, but precision is required. As shown above, boring the hole through the head for the handle is best done on a drill press. Once the mane pieces are glued onto the head, the hole can be bored with a spade bit the same diameter as the dowel that will be used for the handle.

1 Gluing the mane pieces to the head
Once the mane pieces are cut to size *(page 67)*, they can be attached to the head. The mane consists of four pieces: two larger ones located behind the ears and two smaller pieces positioned between the ears and the eyes. Spread glue on the larger pieces and on the mating surfaces of the head, set them in place and, with the head upright on a work surface, clamp them securely *(above)*.

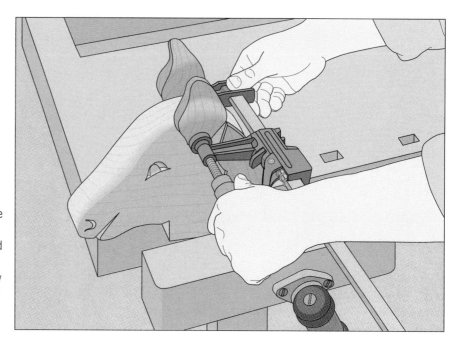

2 Gluing the ears to the head
Mark the location of the handle on the head and bore the hole for it on the drill press *(photo, above)*. Then secure the head in a bench vise and outline the location of the ears on the sides of the head. Apply glue to the contacting surfaces and clamp the ears in place *(right)*. Now glue the smaller mane pieces to the head.

3 **Fastening the head and tail to the body**
Center the head and tail at opposite ends of the body and outline their locations on the board. Then secure the board edge-up in a bench vise and drill countersunk clearance holes through the body within your outlines; bore two holes for the head and one for the tail. Spread glue on the bottom end of the head and within the outline on the body and, holding the head in position on the board, drive the screws through the body and into the head *(right)*. Reposition the body in the vise, and repeat the process to attach the tail.

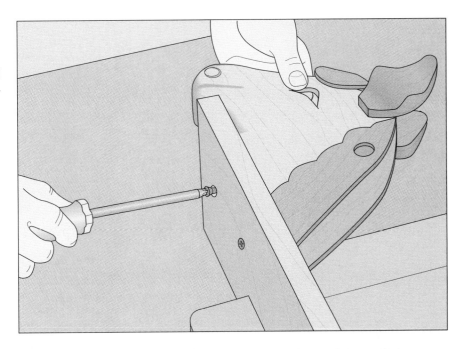

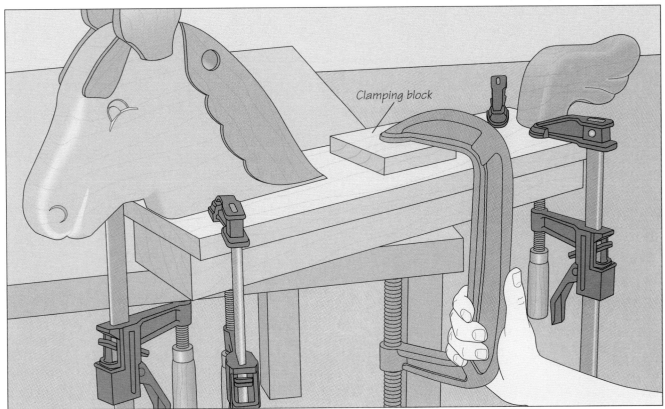

Clamping block

4 **Gluing the body to the leg support board**
Spread glue on the contacting surfaces of the body and the leg support board and center the body on the board. As shown above, use four clamps to hold the pieces together while the adhesive cures. Use a fifth clamp to secure the assembly to a work surface, placing a block under the clamp jaw to distribute the pressure.

MOUNTING THE SADDLE BACK

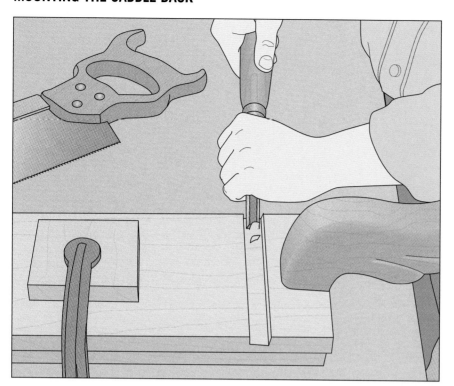

1 Cutting the dado for the saddle back
Clamp the body and leg support board to a work surface, protecting the stock with a wood pad. Cut the saddle back on the band saw *(photo, page 66)* and place it on the body about 1 inch in front of the tail. Tilt the saddle back until it rests against the tail, then outline the location of the piece on the body. Because the dado shoulders must be sloping, cut them with a backsaw. Holding the saw at the same angle at which the saddle back will be tilted, about 15°, cut to a depth of about ½ inch on the back of the dado. Clear the waste with a chisel. Holding the chisel flat-side down, slice through the wood from one end of the dado to the other *(left)*. Make sure the bottom of the dado slopes toward the tail so that the saddle back lies flush with the tail.

2 Gluing the saddle to the body
Prepare a set of clamping blocks for gluing the saddle back in place. Make an arched block with a concave curve the same shape as the top edge of the saddle back and two angled blocks cut with the same angle as the bottom of the dado. Spread glue on the bottom edge of the saddle back and in the dado and clamp the workpiece in place, using the clamping blocks to direct the pressure squarely on the joint *(right)*.

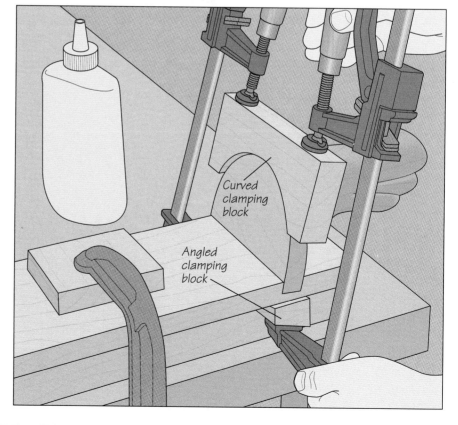

Curved clamping block

Angled clamping block

INSTALLING THE LEGS

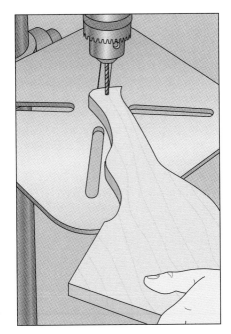

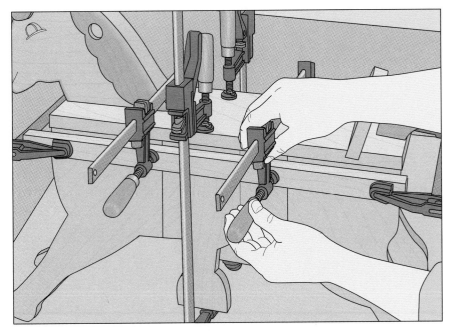

1 Preparing the legs for the metal rods
Before fixing the legs to the body, drill holes into their inside faces for the rods that attach the horse to the stand. Mark the rod locations on the hooves and bore ½-inch-deep holes with a drill press *(above)*, using a brad-point bit the same diameter as the rods.

2 Gluing the leg assemblies to the body
Position each leg-and-stirrup assembly against the body and mark a line along the inside of the assembly where it meets the edge of the body. Then spread glue on the assemblies above your line and on the contacting surfaces of the body and fit the pieces together. With the legs upright on a work surface, install two bar clamps to press the top edges of the assemblies against the underside of the body and four more clamps to secure the assemblies to the sides of the body. Use long wood pads with the second set of clamps to distribute the pressure along the length of both joints *(above)*.

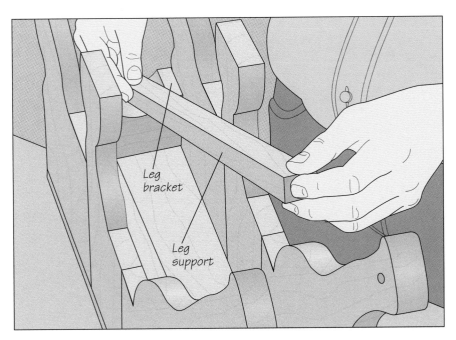

Leg bracket

Leg support

3 Gluing the leg supports and brackets to the body
Referring to the anatomy illustration of the horse *(page 64)*, cut the leg brackets to size. Also saw two leg supports from ¾-inch stock. Spread glue on the contacting surfaces of the pieces and set them in place. As shown at left, the brackets fit between the legs at each end of the body while the supports lie flush against the legs and the underside of the body.

SHAPING THE HORSE

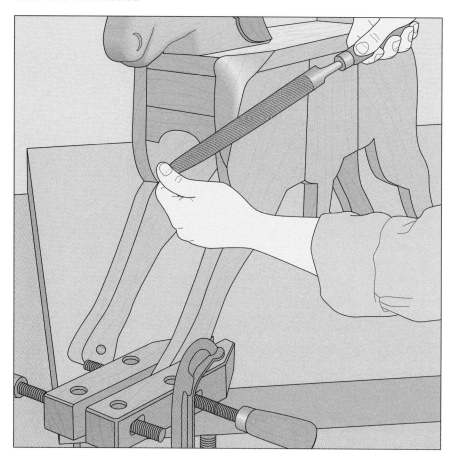

Shaping the body

Secure the horse to a work surface by clamping one leg in a handscrew and clamping the handscrew to the table. Use a rasp to shape the horse's body. Holding the tool with both hands, work from the top of the horse to the bottom to round over the edges of the body and legs *(left)*. Continue until you have smoothed all the sharp edges and corners. Before installing the saddle and halter *(page 75)* or mounting the horse to the stand *(page 76)*, apply a finish to the horse.

ASSEMBLING THE STAND

1 Building the framework

Refer to the anatomy illustration for the dimensions of the stand pieces. Dry-fit the four boards together and mark screw holes on the top and bottom pieces in line with the vertical boards. Drill a counterbored hole at each mark and a pilot hole into the ends of the vertical boards and screw the pieces together. Then fit the stand brackets in the top corners of the stand and mark a screw hole on each side of the corner. Drill counterbored holes and fasten the brackets to the stand *(right)*. Once the pieces are assembled, conceal the screw heads with wood plugs.

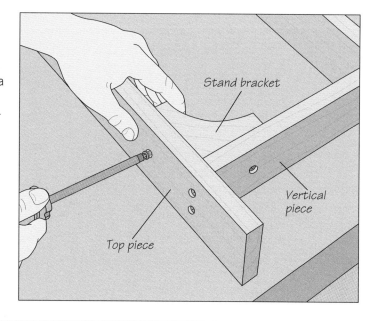

Stand bracket

Vertical piece

Top piece

2 Installing the stand base

The base consists of two boards, one at each end of the stand. With the stand on its side on a work surface, hold one board in position and mark three screw holes on its underside. Use counterbored screws to attach the board to the stand *(right)*. Repeat at the other end of the stand. Paint or finish the stand.

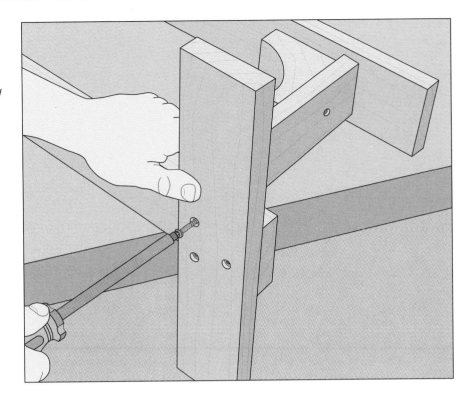

INSTALLING THE SADDLE AND HALTER

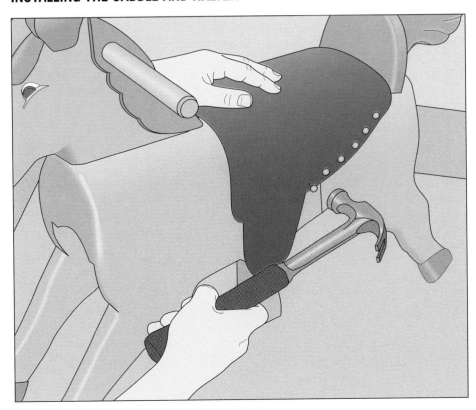

1 Installing the saddle

Cut the saddle to shape from a piece of heavy suede leather, test fit it on the horse, and trim it, if necessary, to make sure it fits between the neck and the saddle back. Spread glue on the underside of the saddle, position it on the horse, and secure the perimeter of the saddle to the body with upholstery tacks spaced at equal intervals *(left)*. Then dab some adhesive in the hole through the mane and insert the dowel that will serve as the handle.

2 Installing the halter
Make the halter from the same suede leather used for the saddle, cutting it into ⅜-inch-wide strips. You will need six strips: two around the top of the head, passing between the ears and mane, two around the jaw, and two more to join these. Test-fit the strips in position, trimming them long enough to loop around the metal rings. Spread glue on the underside of the strips and set them in position on the head. Loop the ends of the strips around the rings and use upholstery tacks to secure them *(right)*.

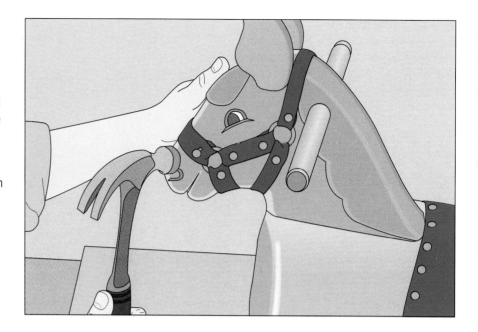

MOUNTING THE HORSE TO THE STAND

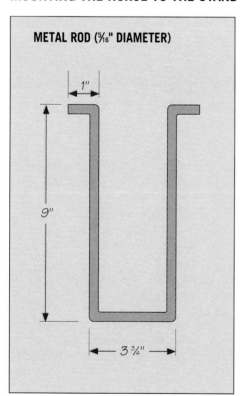

METAL ROD (⁵⁄₁₆" DIAMETER)

1"

9"

3 ¾"

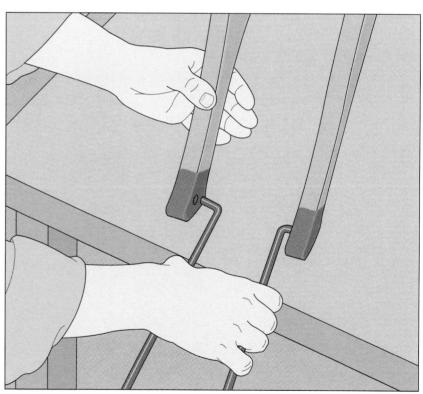

1 Attaching the metal rods to the hooves
Have two ⁵⁄₁₆-inch-diameter metal rods prepared at a metal-working shop to the shape and dimensions shown in the illustration above, at left. Holding the horse upright on a work surface, squeeze one of the rods to fit between the legs *(above, right)* and insert the ends into the holes you drilled in the hooves. Repeat at the other end of the horse.

2 Securing the horse to the stand

Once both rods have been fixed to the horse, prepare the blocks that will secure the rods to the stand. Cut the pieces of wood to size, then saw two ⁵⁄₁₆-inch-long dadoes about ¾ inch from the front end of each block. The dadoes should be the same width as the diameter of the rods. Position the block on the top piece of the stand about ¾ inch from the end and drill counterbored holes through the stand piece and into the block. Place the horse on the stand and, holding the block steady, insert the top of the metal rod into the dadoes in the block. Then fasten the block to the stand from underneath *(right)*. Repeat the process to mount the tail end of the horse to the stand. Do not plug these holes so you can unscrew the block periodically to lubricate the ends of the rods with wax.

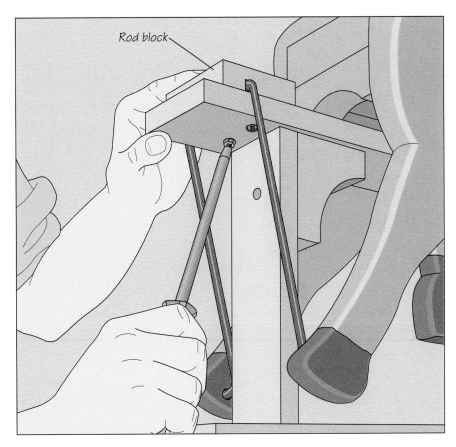

Rod block

3 Installing the footrest

The final step in making the horse is attaching the footrest to the stirrups. With the horse resting on its side on a work surface, position the footrest against the stirrups and drill two counterbored screw holes for each stirrup. If you plan to add wood blocks to the footrest to accommodate a smaller child, drill pilot holes for them into the ends of the foot rest before fastening it to the stirrups. Then, holding the footrest against the stirrups securely, screw the footrest in place *(left)*.

SWINGING HORSE

Designed and built by Fred Sneath of Stony Lake, Ontario, the swinging horse shown at left can be set up indoors or out. The two ropes at the front and the one at the back have rings at the end and can clip onto hooks screwed into ceiling joists. Sneath's version features interchangeable heads.

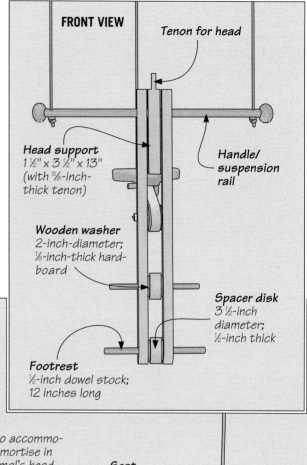

FRONT VIEW

Tenon for head

Head support
1½" x 3½" x 13"
(with ⅝-inch-thick tenon)

Handle/suspension rail

Wooden washer
2-inch-diameter;
⅛-inch-thick hard-board

Spacer disk
3½-inch diameter;
½-inch thick

Footrest
½-inch dowel stock;
12 inches long

ANATOMY OF A SWINGING HORSE

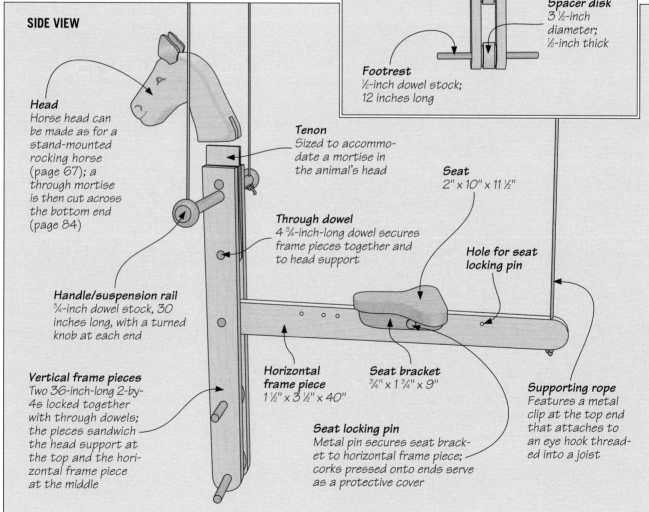

SIDE VIEW

Head
Horse head can be made as for a stand-mounted rocking horse (page 67); a through mortise is then cut across the bottom end (page 84)

Handle/suspension rail
¾-inch dowel stock, 30 inches long, with a turned knob at each end

Vertical frame pieces
Two 36-inch-long 2-by-4s locked together with through dowels; the pieces sandwich the head support at the top and the horizontal frame piece at the middle

Tenon
Sized to accommodate a mortise in the animal's head

Through dowel
4 ¾-inch-long dowel secures frame pieces together and to head support

Horizontal frame piece
1½" x 3½" x 40"

Seat locking pin
Metal pin secures seat bracket to horizontal frame piece; corks pressed onto ends serve as a protective cover

Seat
2" x 10" x 11½"

Hole for seat locking pin

Seat bracket
¾" x 1¾" x 9"

Supporting rope
Features a metal clip at the top end that attaches to an eye hook threaded into a joist

PREPARING THE STOCK

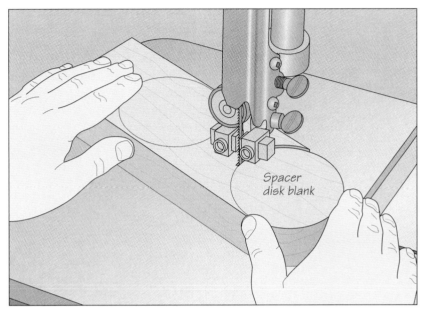

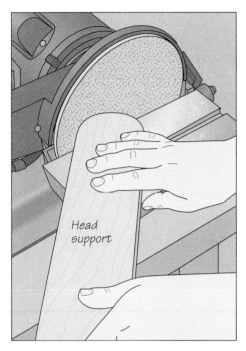

1 Cutting the parts to size
Refer to the anatomy illustrations of the horse on page 78 to size the parts. Make the head from a 2-by-12 as you would for a stand-mounted horse, then cut a through mortise through the bottom end *(page 84)*. Curve the bottom ends of the head support and one end of the frame pieces on your band saw. For the seat, you can use a bicycle seat as a template. To make the spacer disks, use a compass to outline the 3½-inch circles on your blank and cut them out on the band saw *(above)*.

2 Smoothing the stock smooth
Once you have cut all the parts of the horse to size, smooth the edges of the stock with sandpaper or on a spindle sander. Be sure to preserve the rounded end of pieces like the head support *(above)*.

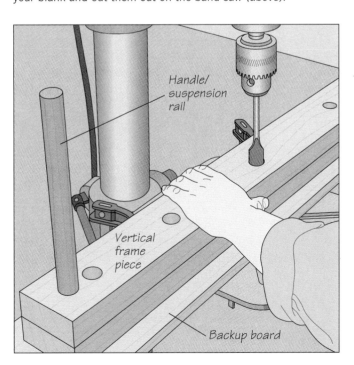

3 Preparing the frame pieces for assembly
Mark holes for the dowels that will join the frame pieces together. On the vertical pieces, mark a hole about 1½ inch from the top, and four more at 8-inch intervals. You will also need to drill a hole about 1½ inch below the top one for the handle. On the horizontal piece, mark the hole 1¾ inch from the front end. Clamp a backup board to your drill press table and set the vertical pieces on top, aligning the edges and ends of the boards. Install a spade bit the same diameter as your dowel stock, then drill the top and bottom holes first so you can use the handle and footrest to keep the boards aligned as you bore the remaining holes *(left)*. To avoid tearout, drill the holes from both sides of the stock. Next, bore the holes in the horizontal piece and the head support, making sure the holes in the support piece and the vertical pieces line up. Use a smaller bit to drill the holes in the horizontal piece for the seat locking pins; refer to the anatomy illustration for the location of these holes. Finally, drill a hole through the edge of the horizontal piece near the back end for the supporting rope.

MOUNTING THE HEAD

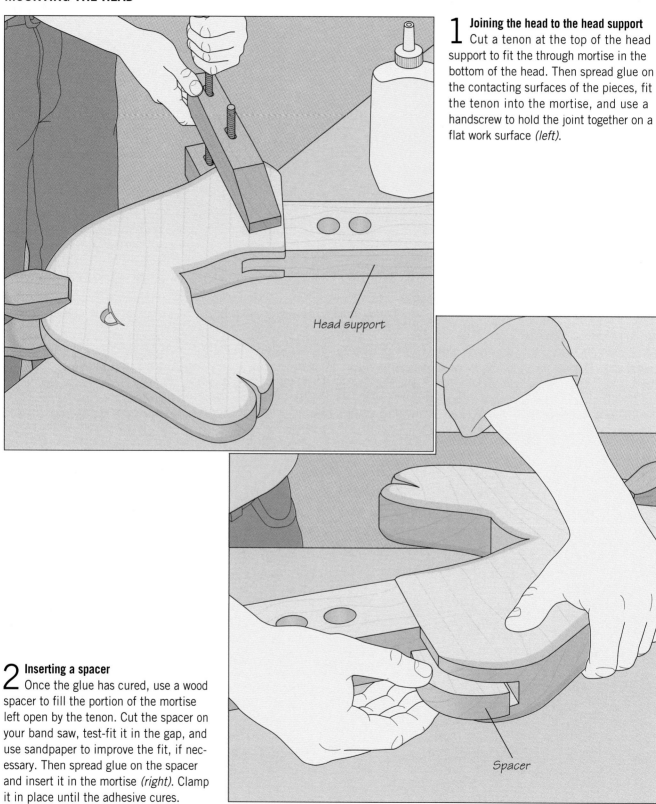

Head support

Spacer

1 Joining the head to the head support
Cut a tenon at the top of the head support to fit the through mortise in the bottom of the head. Then spread glue on the contacting surfaces of the pieces, fit the tenon into the mortise, and use a handscrew to hold the joint together on a flat work surface *(left)*.

2 Inserting a spacer
Once the glue has cured, use a wood spacer to fill the portion of the mortise left open by the tenon. Cut the spacer on your band saw, test-fit it in the gap, and use sandpaper to improve the fit, if necessary. Then spread glue on the spacer and insert it in the mortise *(right)*. Clamp it in place until the adhesive cures.

ASSEMBLING THE HORSE

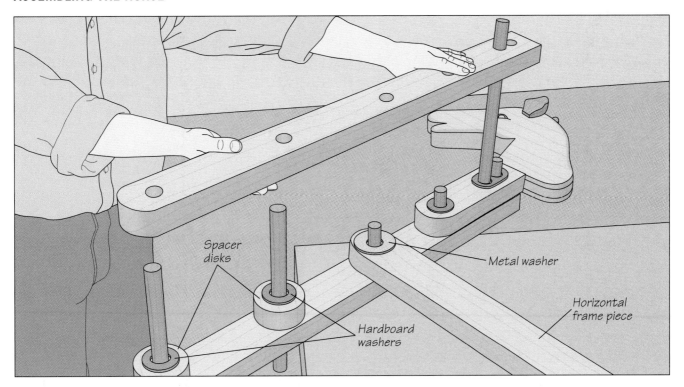

Spacer disks

Hardboard washers

Metal washer

Horizontal frame piece

1 Assembling the frame pieces

Before assembling the horse, cut the ⅛-inch hardboard washers for the joints between the two vertical pieces. Then set one of the vertical pieces on a work surfaces and insert the handle and dowels in their respective holes. Slip a washer around each dowel, then install the head support, the horizontal frame piece, and the circular spacer disks. Add another set of washers and slip the second vertical piece in place *(above)*. Use metal washers for the joint between the vertical and horizontal frame pieces, since this connection must stand up to considerable friction. Once all the pieces are in place, drive a finishing nail through each dowel and into the vertical frame pieces to secure the framework.

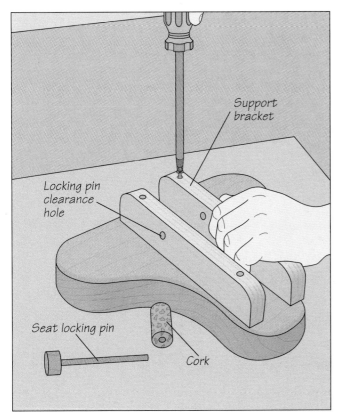

Support bracket

Locking pin clearance hole

Seat locking pin

Cork

2 Installing the seat

Once you have cut the seat and seat brackets to size, drill clearance holes through the brackets for attaching them to both the seat and the horizontal frame piece. Screw the brackets to the underside of the seat *(left)*, then use the locking pin to secure the seat to the framework. To cover the sharp ends of the pin, glue a wooden pad to one end and push a cork onto the other end once the seat in in place.

TRADITIONAL ROCKING HORSE

A deft stroke from an artist's brush applies the finishing touch to an eye of the rocking horse shown at right. A good part of the appeal of a wooden toy depends on careful finishing. The runners, cross braces, and footrest of this horse were coated with pure tung oil. The rest of the horse was finished with nontoxic paint: four coats of black paint on the entire body, then two coats of white paint to bring out details like the tail, mane, eyes, nostrils, and mouth.

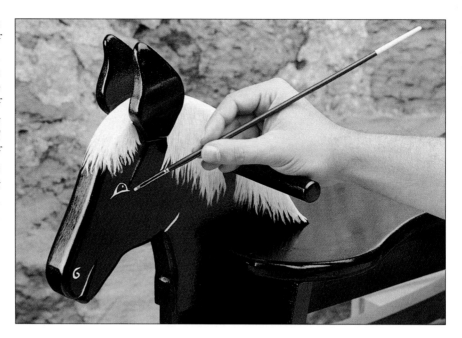

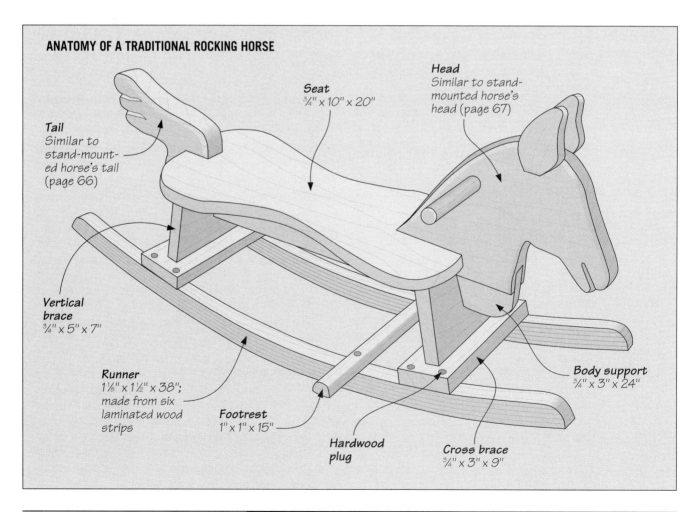

ANATOMY OF A TRADITIONAL ROCKING HORSE

Tail
Similar to stand-mount-ed horse's tail (page 66)

Seat
¾" x 10" x 20"

Head
Similar to stand-mounted horse's head (page 67)

Vertical brace
¾" x 5" x 7"

Runner
1⅛" x 1½" x 38"; made from six laminated wood strips

Footrest
1" x 1" x 15"

Hardwood plug

Cross brace
¾" x 3" x 9"

Body support
¾" x 3" x 24"

ASSEMBLING THE HORSE

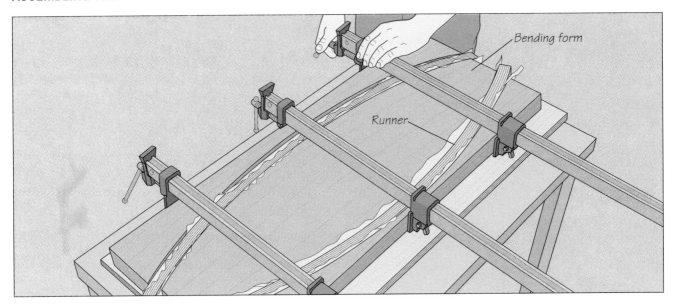

1 Bending and laminating the runners

Use a bending form to give the runners their curved shape and glue up the pieces of the laminations. For the form, adjust trammel points to a radius of 45 inches and mark two arcs near opposite edges of a 2-by-12 plank. Cut along both lines on your band saw, then make parallel cuts on the outside pieces, to accommodate the 1⅛ inch thickness of the runners. Screw the middle piece of the form to a plywood base, then prepare the runner stock. Rip twelve ³⁄₁₆-inch-thick strips from a 1½-inch-wide piece

of hardwood with good bending qualities, like ash. Line the edges of the form with wax paper to prevent the lamination from sticking to the form. Then spread glue on one side of each strip and butt six of them together against each edge of the form. Press the outside pieces of the form against the strips to bend them slightly. Bend and secure the lamination with bar clamps *(above)*. Let the laminations cure for 8 to 10 hours, then joint the edges of the runners and round their ends on the band saw.

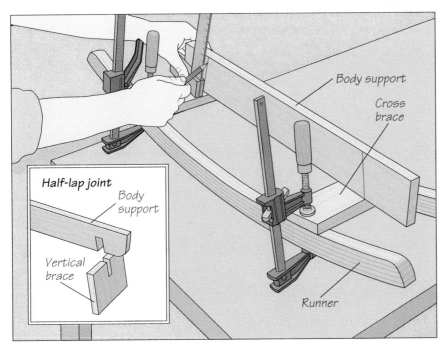

Half-lap joint
Body support
Vertical brace

2 Bending and laminating the runners

Before assembling the horse, test-fit the pieces together and mark the edge half-laps that join the body support to the vertical braces *(inset)*. Clamp the cross braces to the runners about 6 inches from each end. Then, with the body support centered on the braces, use a try square to mark lines on the body support perpendicular to the top of each brace *(left)*. Use the thickness of the vertical braces to add another set of lines parallel to the first two; these lines outline the half-laps. Cut the edges of the half-laps halfway across the width of the body support on the band saw and remove the waste pieces with a chisel. Use the half-laps in the body support to mark the mating half-laps in the vertical braces, then make the cuts. Curve the bottom ends of the support board on the band saw and sand all surfaces.

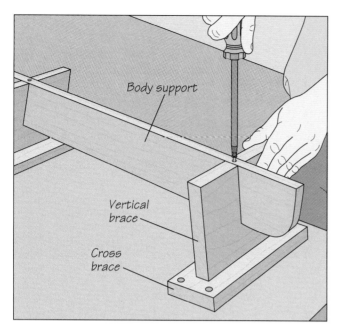

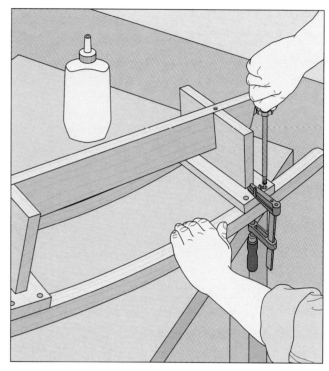

3 Attaching the body support to the braces

Once the half-laps are finished, unclamp the cross braces from the runners, dry-fit the body support and vertical braces together, and position the pieces on the cross braces. Mark and drill counterbored screw holes on the top edge of the body support in line with the vertical braces, on the bottom face of the cross braces in line with the vertical braces, and near the corners of the cross braces in line with the runners. Spread glue in the half-laps, then screw the braces together and attach the body support to the vertical braces *(above)*.

4 Installing the runners

Apply glue to the underside of the cross braces in line with the runners and clamp the runners in position. Using the counterbored holes in the braces as a guide, drill pilot holes into the runners and screw them in place *(above)*. Glue in hardwood plugs cut from a contrasting hardwood to cover all the screw heads.

5 Preparing the head and tail

Before shaping the head and tail *(pages 68 and 69)*, use your table saw to cut the through mortises that will join them to the body support. To steady the stock during the cut, clamp a featherboard to the saw table in line with the blade; brace the featherboard with a support piece and shim the featherboard to keep the workpiece from wobbling. Align the center of the leading end of the blank with the saw blade, butt the rip fence against the workpiece, and make the cut. Turn the workpiece end-for-end, shift the fence away from the blade by the thickness of the kerf, and repeat the cut. Continue widening the dado this way *(right)* until the blank fits properly on the body support.

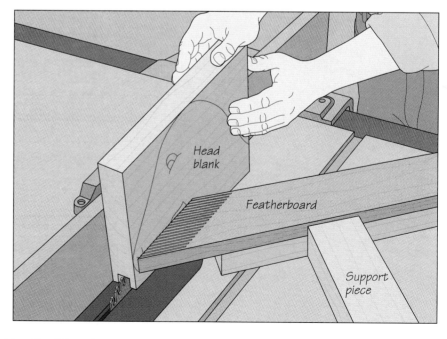

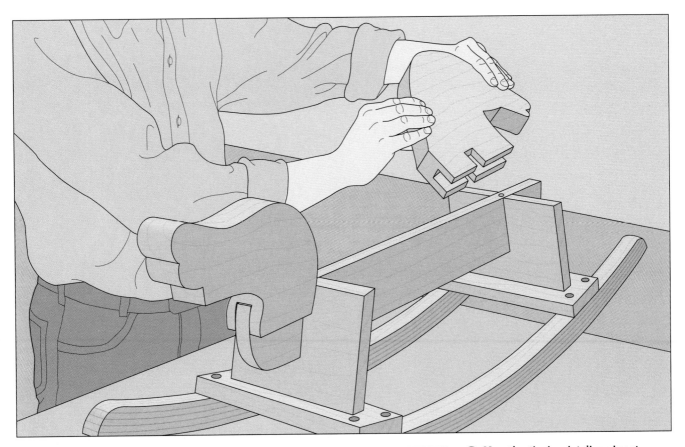

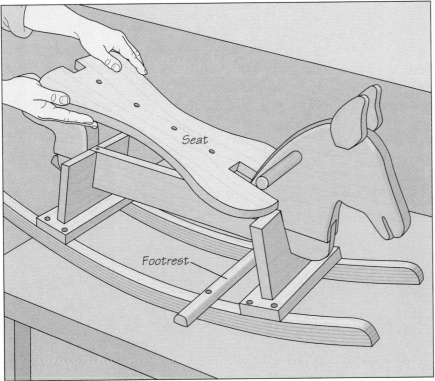

6 Mounting the head, tail, and seat
Test-fit the head blank on the horse, outline the location of the vertical brace on it, and cut the notch on your band saw. Shape the tail and head as you would for a stand-mounted horse *(page 68)* and glue ears to the sides of the head. Bore a hole through the head for a dowel handle *(page 70)* and glue it in place. Then spread glue in the notches in the tail and head, and position them on the body support *(above)*. Next, cut the seat to size, sand its surfaces smooth, and position it on the body support. Outline notches on the seat for the head and tail, then cut them on the band saw. Cut the footrest, round over its ends with sandpaper, and screw it to the runners, again counterboring the fasteners. Set the seat in place *(left)* and fasten it to the body support with counterbored screws. To complete the assembly, cover the screw heads with hardwood plugs.

DOLLHOUSES

The interior of a dollhouse can be made as lifelike as your woodworking skills and patience allow. The interior shown above, built by Carlo Zappa of Montreal, Quebec, comes complete with mini-furnishings, family photos, and other memorabilia.

A well-built dollhouse can survive for as long as an actual dwelling and entertain generations of youngsters—and adults. This chapter will show you how to put the finishing touches on the type of dollhouse you can build from a kit. The emphasis is on producing a realistic and entertaining house, one that will be sufficiently well-designed and sturdy to withstand the only real hazard to which it will have to endure: the busy hands of its owner.

Building and adding accessories to a dollhouse require a unique skill—the ability to work in miniature. The chapter will examine the most important considerations, including scale modeling and using specialized dollhouse-making tools *(page 89)*, wiring the interior so that lighting can be installed *(page 90)*, and adding interior flooring and roofing shingles *(page 92)*.

As with any woodworking project, proper planning and preparation are essential. Keep a few tips in mind. If you are using a kit, be sure to read the instructions before removing the parts from their packaging. The components usually come in sheets of stock that must be sanded on both sides with a 200-grit wet/dry paper; for best results, use an orbital sander. Also sand the edges of the individual parts once they are removed from their sheets so they will fit together cleanly. And before gluing up the parts, test-assemble them with tape and make any necessary adjustments before applying adhesive.

Decide how you you will finish and paint the dollhouse before you try assembling it. It is a good idea to paint the trim, for example, before installing it. Use fast-drying acrylic paint rather than oil-based products. And remember to sand painted surfaces between coats, to smooth any raised grain, ensuring that the next coat adheres properly. Lastly, wood surfaces should be painted on both sides; otherwise they may end up warping.

Except for its miniature scale, a classic dollhouse, like The Jefferson model shown at left, could almost pass for the real thing. Available in kit form, this project includes doors, windows, shutters, siding, and a shingle roof.

ANATOMY OF A DIE-CUT DOLLHOUSE

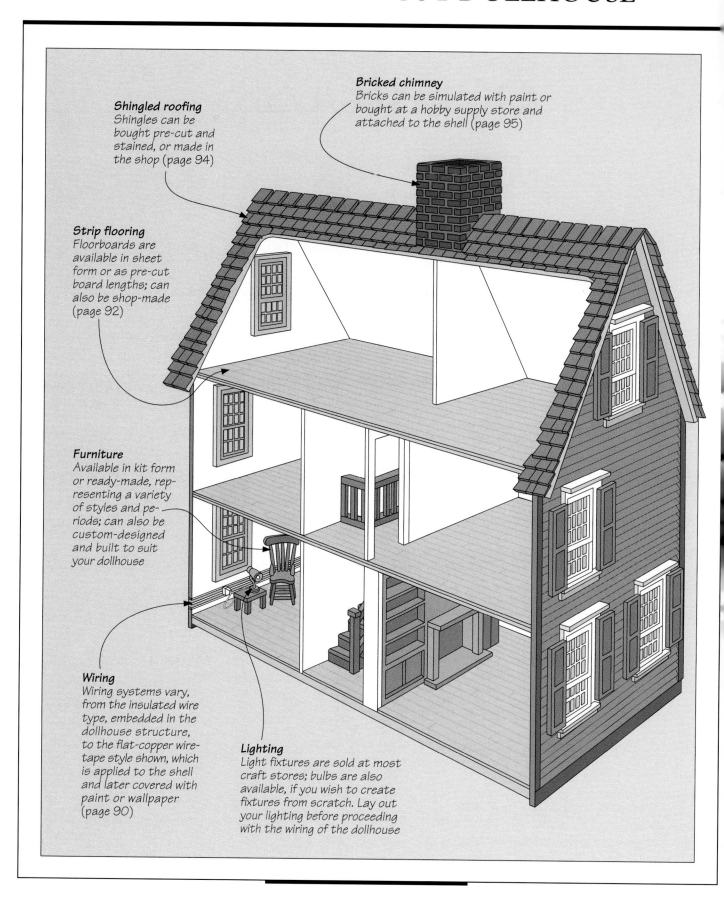

Bricked chimney
Bricks can be simulated with paint or bought at a hobby supply store and attached to the shell (page 95)

Shingled roofing
Shingles can be bought pre-cut and stained, or made in the shop (page 94)

Strip flooring
Floorboards are available in sheet form or as pre-cut board lengths; can also be shop-made (page 92)

Furniture
Available in kit form or ready-made, representing a variety of styles and periods; can also be custom-designed and built to suit your dollhouse

Wiring
Wiring systems vary, from the insulated wire type, embedded in the dollhouse structure, to the flat-copper wire-tape style shown, which is applied to the shell and later covered with paint or wallpaper (page 90)

Lighting
Light fixtures are sold at most craft stores; bulbs are also available, if you wish to create fixtures from scratch. Lay out your lighting before proceeding with the wiring of the dollhouse

Once the shell of your dollhouse has been assembled, the decorative elements can be installed. This is one of the most challenging parts of the project. Period furniture, individualized rooms, wallpaper and decorations, lighting, customized window frames, and doorways all enhance a dollhouse's appeal. Whether or not these elements are custom-made, assembled from a kit, or selected from ready-made objects, they can mirror the tastes and creative impulses of the maker.

Customizing a dollhouse can involve investing in some specialized equipment. But no special skills—other than patience and time—are required. If the thought of copying a real-life object seems too challenging, you can refer to one of the many dollhouse enthusiasts' publications available. These are an excellent source of information on specific projects; many also provide tips on recreating objects using readily available items, as described in the Shop Tip below. Many publications also include plans, scaled to miniature, for reproducing furniture and other decorative items, like the chair shown at right.

The main concern in building objects in miniature is choosing an appropriate texture for the materials you are using. Wood grain must be tight and fabric designs small enough in scale to realistically represent the object in miniature. The small stock needed is readily available from hobby supply shops, but many parts can be salvaged. The listing at right details some of the tools required for miniature work.

Smaller than a child's hand, the stick chair shown above can give a dollhouse a warm, lived-in appearance.

A DOLLHOUSE TOOL KIT

The following is a list of common and specialized tools needed to build and decorate a dollhouse:

- Small and large scissors for cutting sheets of wood and fabric

- Tweezers (pointed and angled) for holding small parts and steadying brads for hammering

- Toothpicks for spreading glue into tight spots

- Straight pins for holding parts in position before gluing

- Artist's brushes (several sizes) for painting details and applying glue

- Glue syringe for injecting adhesive into hard-to-reach places

- Pencil for scribing layout and cutting lines

- Ruler for measuring and marking straight edges

- Craft knife with No. 11 blades for cutting thin materials

- Wire cutter or nail clippers for making custom parts from metal and trimming wires

- Needle-nose pliers for holding small parts during assembly and punching pilot holes for brads

- Small hammer for driving brads

- Masking tape and transparent tape for holding parts while glue is curing

- Emery board for filing edges and sizing parts

- Mini-miter box and saw for cutting miniature trim and molding

- Small C clamps and clothes pins for holding stock during glue up

- Pin vise drill for penetrating dollhouse shell and making pilot holes for brads

- Single-edge razor blades for cutting precise edges

- Wax paper and rags for clean up

SHOP TIP

A shop-made sink
A dollhouse version of a porcelain sink for a kitchen or bathroom can be made from a clean plastic jelly or butter container. Paint the tub white, then trim the lip a little, apply some glue under the edge, and insert the tub in the countertop.

CUSTOMIZING A DOLLHOUSE

Once the shell of a dollhouse is assembled, the next step is planning the design of its interior and exterior. This section will show you how to install a wiring system, wood flooring, and roofing shingles.

A backsaw in a mini-miter box cuts a piece of window trim to length. Like other scale-size tools needed for dollhouse-building, the box and saw are available at most hobby shops.

Wiring a dollhouse is easy if you use a lighting kit. The type shown below uses double-copper-band tape with adhesive backing. The step-by-step procedures that follow will work with most commercial kits.

There are many ways to install flooring in a dollhouse. Carpet-style flooring, made with a suitable fabric that has the texture of carpeting in a miniature scale, is one popular choice. You can also buy sheets of flooring that look much like wood floors; these feature an adhesive backing. As shown beginning on page 92, a third option involves making and installing your own customized wood floorboards.

The roof can be covered with pre-cut shingles, available at most hobby shops. Before buying shingles, measure the total surface area of the roof and add 25 percent to take into account the overlap of shingles. Purchase extra shingles to allow for waste. As with floors, you can make your own shingles in the shop, as explained starting on page 94.

INSTALLING LIGHTING

1 Installing the tape wiring
Start by drawing a layout—or wiring diagram—of the dollhouse interior, marking the locations of light fixtures, outlets, junctions, and any anticipated future additions. Then transfer the diagram to the surface of the interior with a pencil. Make sure your arrangement conforms to the instructions included in the installation manual supplied with the wiring kit. In the case of a double-copper-band tape wiring system, for example, the wiring run must start ½ inch from the edge of an outside wall to allow room for the junction splice to be installed. Run the tape around the corner and into the interior *(right)*, pressing it into place on the walls. Once the first line has been mounted on the inside wall, stop and attach the splice junction *(step 2)*.

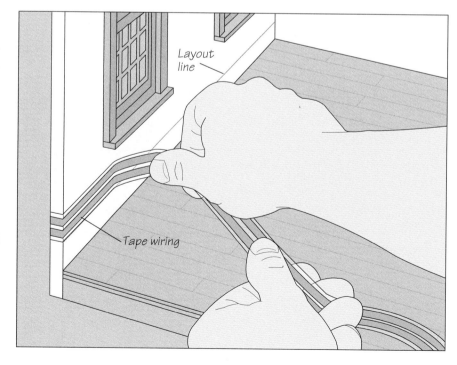

Layout line

Tape wiring

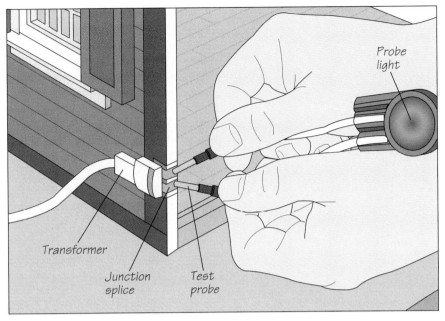

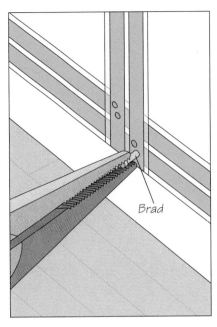

2 Testing the wiring

Attach the junction splice supplied with the kit to the wiring by pressing it onto the copper tape on the outside wall of the dollhouse. Secure the junction to the wall with a small wood screw. Next, check the conductivity of the wiring to ensure sufficient voltage is running through it. Plug the lead wire into the junction and the transformer at the other end of the wire into a wall outlet. Then, touch the leads of the test probe supplied to the copper foils beside the junction *(above)*. The light should come on; if not, make sure that the lead wire switch is turned on. If it is, refer to the owner's manual for instructions on troubleshooting the transformer.

3 Extending the wiring upward

To extend the wiring up a wall to the ceiling or the upper floor, lap a piece of wiring at a 90° angle over the run already installed on the wall. To secure the connection, use needle-nose pliers to push two pairs of brads through both sets of wiring into the wall *(above)*. Test the new run as you did in step 2.

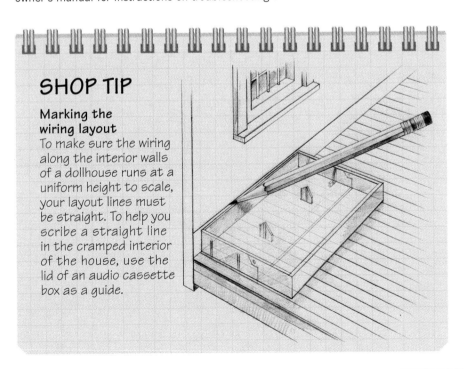

SHOP TIP

Marking the wiring layout
To make sure the wiring along the interior walls of a dollhouse runs at a uniform height to scale, your layout lines must be straight. To help you scribe a straight line in the cramped interior of the house, use the lid of an audio cassette box as a guide.

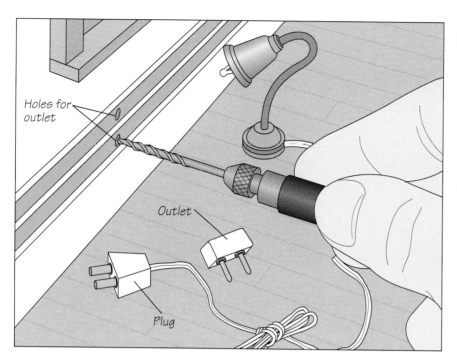

Holes for outlet

Outlet

Plug

4 Installing lighting fixtures
A light fixture can be installed at any point along the wiring. To connect a fixture without a plug, use a pin to punch small holes into the copper tape large to accept the lead wires from the fixture. Insert the wires into the holes, then secure the wires in place with brass brads. For a fixture with a plug, like the one shown at left, you will need to fix an outlet to the wiring. Drill or punch holes into the tape for the outlet prongs, press the prongs in place, and insert the fixture plug into the outlet.

INSTALLING FLOORING

1 Ripping the floor boards
Cut your flooring stock to length and plane it to a thickness of ¼ inch. Because you will be cutting the boards ⅛ inch wide, make a special table saw insert for this operation. (If you use the insert supplied with the saw, the narrow boards could jam in the saw table, resulting in kickback.) To make an insert that will minimize the gap between the blade and the table opening, use the standard insert as a template to cut a blank from a piece of wood of the same thickness. Crank the blade to its lowest setting and set the new insert in place. Position the rip fence to straddle the insert, making sure that it is not directly above the blade. Then turn on the saw and raise the blade to a height of ¼ inch, cutting a slot in the insert. To rip the floor boards, position the rip fence for a cutting width of ⅛ inch and use a push block to feed the workpiece across the saw table, pressing the stock flush against the fence with your free hand *(right)*.

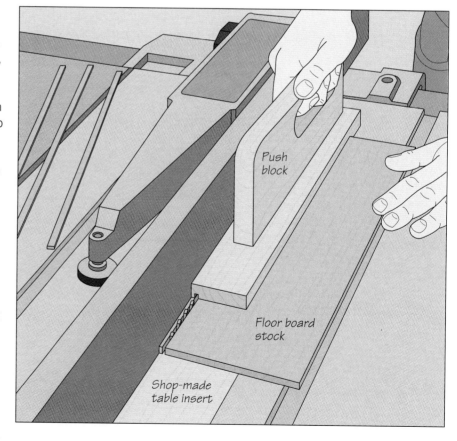

Push block

Floor board stock

Shop-made table insert

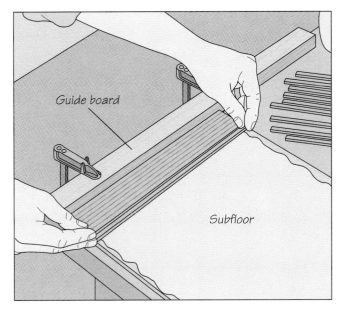

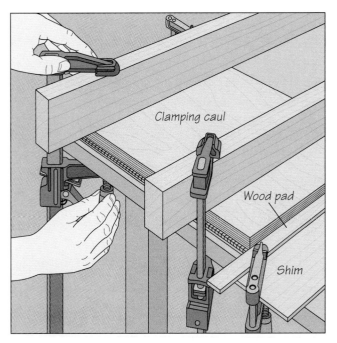

2 Gluing down the floor boards
Once your boards are cut, glue them down to a subfloor before installing the flooring in the dollhouse. For the subfloor, use ¹⁄₁₆-inch model aircraft plywood, available at most craft supply stores. Cut a piece larger than the floor, set it on a work surface, and outline the floor on it. Clamp a guide board along each end of the outline, then spread an even coating of glue on the subfloor within the outline. Starting at one end, position a floor board on the subfloor, butting one edge against the guide board and making sure the ends are aligned with the outline. Continue gluing down the boards edge to edge (above) until you reach the other guide board.

3 Securing the floor boards
Once the last floor board is glued down, remove the guide boards and place a piece of plywood at least as large as the floor on top of it. Place two 2-by-4s on top of the plywood, making sure the plywood caul is perfectly flat on the floor. To keep the floor boards butted edge to edge, cut two ¹⁄₈-inch-thick wood pads as long as the floor is wide, butt them tightly against the edges of the floor on shims as thick as the subfloor, and clamp them to the work surface. Then clamp the caul in place, using the 2-by-4s to distribute the clamping pressure (above).

SHOP TIP

Laying out irregular floors
If the floors of your dollhouse have an irregular shape, you can use sheets of paper to map out the flooring. Lay individual pieces of paper on the floor, trimming them to fit precisely within the walls, and tape the pieces together. Next, remove the paper template from the dollhouse, set it on top of the subfloor material, and trace its outline. Then cut the subfloor to size on a scroll saw or band saw.

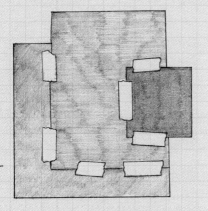

INSTALLING SHINGLES

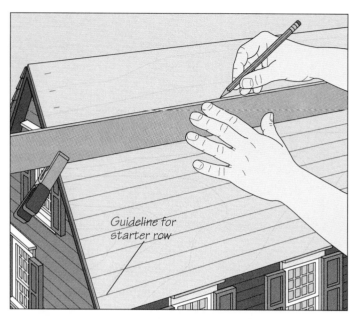

Guideline for starter row

1 Laying out the roofing
To make sure the shingles are installed straight and with the desired amount of overlap, mark guidelines for them on the roof. Position a shingle in a bottom corner of the roof with the amount of overhang you want; ¼ inch is adequate. Then mark a guideline for the starter row along the top end of the shingle. Holding the first shingle in place, position another above it—overlapping the first—and mark a second guideline the same way. Use the spacing between the two marks to draw a series of pencil ticks up the roof to the ridge. Repeat the process at the opposite corner and at both ends on the other side of the roof, then use a straight-edge and a pencil to join the marks, forming guidelines for installing the shingles. Clamp the straightedge to the roof at both corresponding marks as you draw each line *(left)*.

BUILT IT YOURSELF

SHINGLE-CUTTING JIG
Made from wood scraps, the guillotine-like jig shown at right is ideal for making your own shingles. Start by sawing the guide block and blade guide. Cut a dado out of the guide to fit the plane blade you will use, then screw the guide to the block. Rout a dado through the assembly to accommodate your shingle stock, screw on the base, then make the stop block, beveling one edge. The distance between the stop block's beveled edge and the opening in the guide block equals the desired thickness of the shingles.

To use the jig, slip a plane blade, bevel facing out, into the blade guide and slide vertical-grained shingle stock through the opening until it contacts the stop block.

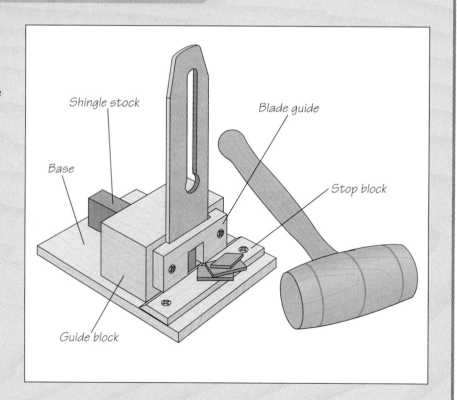

Shingle stock

Blade guide

Base

Stop block

Guide block

2 Gluing down the shingles

Install one row of shingles at a time. Spread glue between the starter guideline and the bottom of the roof, and set the shingles in place, aligning the top end with the guideline. Adjoining shingles should butt together edge to edge. Glue down each row of shingles the same way *(above)*.

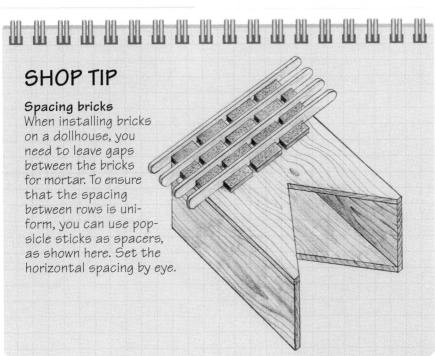

SHOP TIP

Spacing bricks

When installing bricks on a dollhouse, you need to leave gaps between the bricks for mortar. To ensure that the spacing between rows is uniform, you can use popsicle sticks as spacers, as shown here. Set the horizontal spacing by eye.

GAMES AND PUZZLES

The 3-D puzzle shown above was produced on a band saw by Ray Levy of Soquel, California. The secret to a good solid-wood puzzle lies in planning the saw cuts. The pieces must slide apart easily yet present an interesting challenge to reassemble. To minimize the width of the kerfs between the pieces, it is best to use the thinnest blade that will do the job.

As a toy maker, you do not need to limit your creations to a young audience. The games and puzzles featured in this chapter will captivate adults and children alike—without causing you much expense. Most games and puzzles can be fashioned from wood scraps left over from other projects.

As shown beginning on page 98, a chessboard can be glued up from strips of contrasting wood, such as ash and walnut, cut from two boards. The 32 chessmen needed for the game can be turned on a lathe from small blanks. The cribbage board illustrated on page 105 was produced from a piece of purpleheart left over from another project. And the layered jigsaw puzzle featured in the photo on page 108 was assembled from small bits of different-colored hardwoods, including bubinga, walnut, and wenge.

The making of wooden games and puzzles has a long history. In 1760, English craftsman John Spillsbury created what he called "dissected maps for the teaching of geography" by gluing maps to thin sheets of mahogany and cutting out the features for his lessons. As shown starting on page 108, you can apply Spillsbury's techniques to produce jigsaw puzzles out of paper and wood. In fact, you can produce a puzzle illustrating virtually any image that can be rendered on paper, from postcards and road maps to place mats and color photocopies. Just glue the paper onto a wood base and cut the puzzle on a band saw or scroll saw.

The projects described on the following pages can be as simple or as challenging as your woodworking skills allow. The chessmen illustrated on page 102, for example, are fairly easy to turn on the lathe, but you can make them as elaborate as you like. Similarly, a basic cribbage board can be embellished by adding contrasting veneer inlay to the base wood before drilling the peg holes. And as you become more proficient at cutting out jigsaw puzzles, you can tackle projects that feature smaller pieces, creating more elaborate results.

The all-wood chessboard shown at left was assembled from alternating strips of ash and walnut, and mounted in a walnut frame. The piece shown, a 6-inch-high king, was turned by woodworker Michael Mode of New Haven, Vermont.

CHESSBOARD AND CHESSMEN

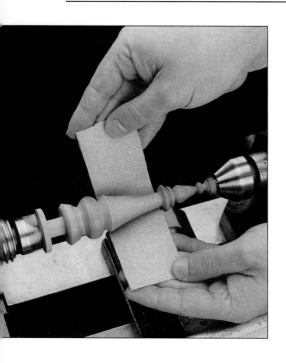

The traditional method for constructing a chessboard involves inlaying square veneers of contrasting wood onto a substrate. The technique shown on the following pages is simpler to execute, but the results are comparable. Start by ripping eight strips of contrasting wood and edge-gluing them together *(below)*. Then crosscut the panel into strips again and reglue the alternating dark-and-light pieces together to form the familiar checkered pattern *(page 99)*.

For your stock, choose any two species that contrast visually, such as ash and walnut. Cut the boards about 50 percent longer than the finished size of the chessboard, plane them to a thickness of ½ inch and rip them into strips 1½ to 3 inches wide, depending on your board's final dimensions. To avoid having to joint the edges of the strips, do the ripping with a combination blade on your table saw.

Once the board is glued up and mounted, you can turn your attention to turning the chessmen. Patterns and procedures for producing the various pieces are presented starting on page 102.

A small strip of sandpaper smooths a bishop still mounted between centers on a lathe. For best results, switch on the lathe, hold the paper in both hands, and lift it against the workpiece from underneath.

MAKING A CHESSBOARD

1 Gluing up the strips
Set your bar clamps on a work surface and lay the strips on them, alternating dark and light pieces. Use as many clamps as necessary to support the stock at 24- to 36-inch intervals. Mark the end grain orientation of each strip, then experiment with the arrangement of the strips until you have a visually pleasing pattern, making sure that the end grain of adjacent boards runs in opposite directions. This will help keep the chessboard from warping. Next, mark a triangle on the strips to help you arrange them correctly should you move them prior to glue up. Standing the strips on edge, spread glue on each one. Butt the strips together and align them, then tighten the clamps to close the joints; use wood pads to protect the stock. Place a third clamp across the top of the strips, centering it between the two underneath. Keeping the assembly as flat as possible *(right)*, tighten all the clamps until there are no gaps between the boards and a thin glue bead squeezes out of the joints.

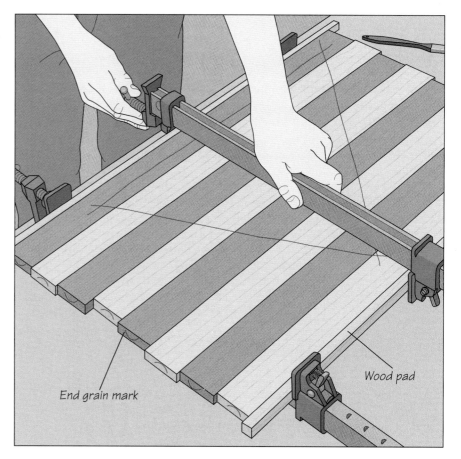

End grain mark

Wood pad

2 Crosscutting the panel into strips

Once the glue has cured, you are ready to crosscut the glued-up panel into strips of alternating light and dark squares. To prevent the panel from lifting off the saw table during the cut, feed it using a jig *(inset)*. Make the device from ½-inch plywood, cutting the base with a lip at one end. Fasten the hold-down to the base so it overhangs the lipped edge by about 2 inches. Lastly, screw a push stick-type handle to the hold-down at the jig's trailing end. To set the cutting width, butt the straight edge of the jig against the rip fence and position the fence so the strips will be exactly the same width as the first series you cut. Holding the jig flush against the fence and the panel square in the jig's notch, cut the strips. Use one hand to push the jig forward and the other to steady the board *(right)*. Cut a few extra strips to give you more flexibility at glue-up time *(step 3)*.

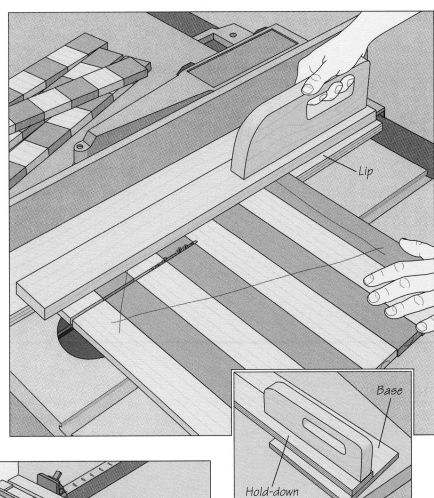

3 Making the chessboard

Glue the crosscut strips together with bar clamps as in step 1. Use two clamps underneath the strips and tighten them, protecting the stock with wood pads. To keep the edges of the strips aligned, place two more clamps across the top of the stock, arranging them at a 90° angle to the two underneath. Again, use wood pads. Since you are gluing end grain to end grain, the glue bond is only needed to hold the strips together until the chessboard is mounted to a substrate panel *(step 5)*. Holding the strips down flat, apply enough clamping pressure to butt the mating surface together with a minimal amount of glue squeeze out *(left)*.

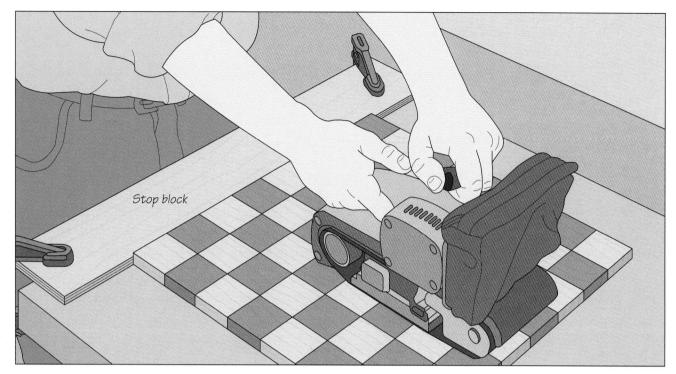

Stop block

4 Leveling and smoothing the chessboard

Use a belt sander to make the top surface of the chess-board perfectly flat and smooth. To keep the board from moving as you sand it, clamp a plywood stop block to your work surface. Install an 80-grit sanding belt in the tool and set the board down so you will be sanding across the grain. Make a few passes across the entire surface, using straight, smooth, overlapping strokes; avoid sweeping the sander in a circular fashion. Then turn the board around and repeat. Once the surface is flat, repeat the process, sanding diagonal to the grain and a final time with the grain *(above)*. Turn the workpiece over and sand the other side the same way.

5 Mounting the chessboard to a substrate

Use ¾-inch plywood for the substrate panel, cutting it ⅛ inch wider and longer than the chessboard to allow for expansion and contraction of the solid-wood board. Spread glue on the underside of the chessboard and the top surface of the substrate and press the two pieces together, centering the chessboard on the panel. To hold the board in place while you install the clamps, drive two small screws through the substrate into the chessboard. Make sure the fasteners do not split the board or penetrate its top surface. Set the assembly astride a sawhorse, using C clamps to secure the board and substrate together. Use wood cauls to distribute the clamping pressure evenly *(right)*.

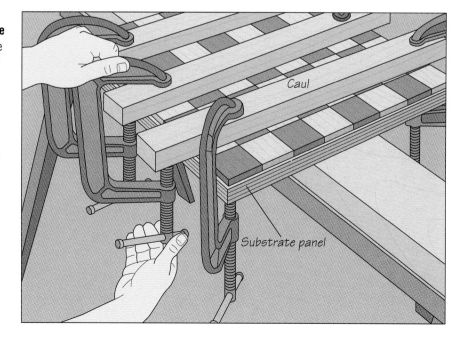

Caul

Substrate panel

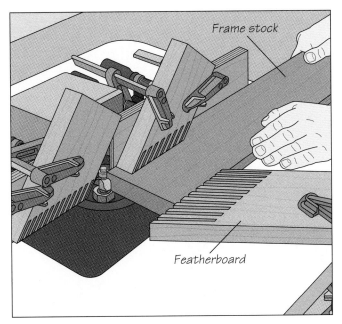

Frame stock

Featherboard

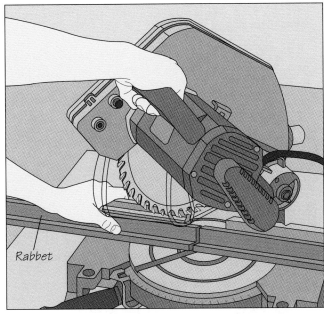

Rabbet

6 Making a frame for the chessboard

Make the frame from a 4½-inch-wide board slightly more than twice as long as the chessboard. Start by shaping both edges of the frame stock. Install a piloted molding bit in your router and mount the tool in a table. Align the fences with the bit pilot and use three featherboards to support the stock during the cut: Clamp two to the fence, one on each side of the cutter, and a third to the table. Hold the workpiece flush against the fence as you shape each edge (above, left). Finish the cut with a push stick. Rip a 1-inch-wide strip from each edge of the stock, then plow a rabbet into the straight edge of each piece. Make the depth of the rabbet equal to the combined thickness of the chessboard and substrate, and its width ½ inch. Finally, cut the frame pieces to length, mitering the ends with a hand saw or a power miter saw (above, right).

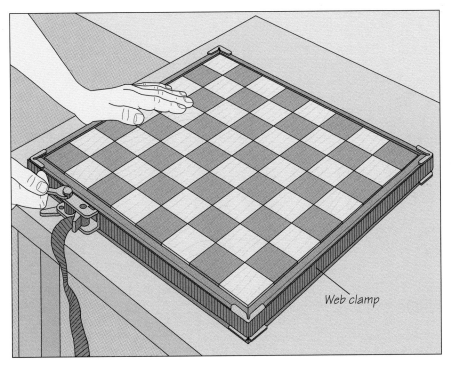

Web clamp

7 Mounting the frame to the chessboard

Start by gluing the frame pieces together. Apply glue on the mitered ends and fit them together, using the chessboard as a form and being careful not to spread any adhesive on the chessboard or substrate. Hold the frame together with a web clamp (left). Once the adhesive has cured, spread glue in the rabbets in the frame only where the frame will contact the substrate. Set the chessboard and substrate in the frame and clamp the assembly together. Finish-sand the chessboard with a random-orbit sander fitted with a fine-grit disk.

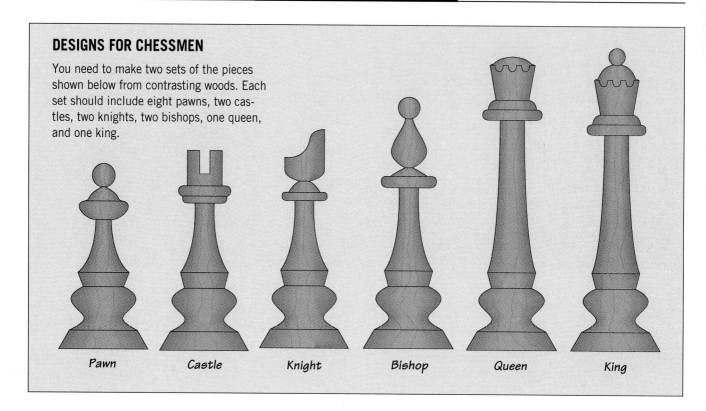

DESIGNS FOR CHESSMEN

You need to make two sets of the pieces shown below from contrasting woods. Each set should include eight pawns, two castles, two knights, two bishops, one queen, and one king.

| Pawn | Castle | Knight | Bishop | Queen | King |

MAKING CHESSMEN

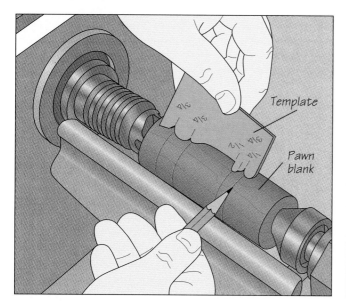

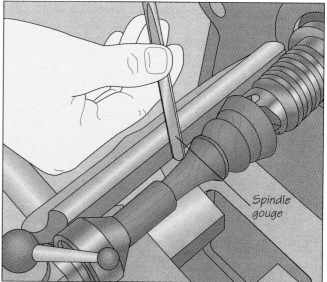

1 Turning the pieces

To produce a chessman on your lathe, transfer the pattern *(above, top)* to a hardboard template, cut it out and mark the diameter of each element in the turning—V-cuts, urns, and beads—on the template. Mount a blank between centers on the machine and use a roughing gouge to turn the piece into a cylinder. Then, holding the edge of the template against the blank, use a pencil to transfer the layout lines to the workpiece *(above, left)*. For the pawn shown, make the V-cuts with a skew chisel, then use a small spindle gouge to turn the urn and beads *(above, right)*.

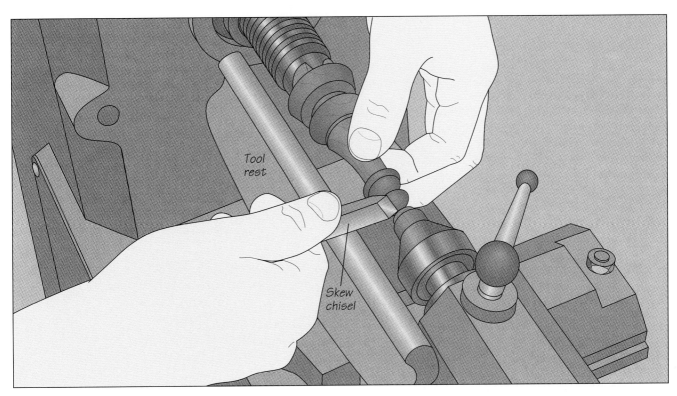

Tool rest

Skew chisel

2 Parting off the chessman

Once you have turned the piece, smooth its surface with sandpaper *(photo, page 98)*, then part it off from the lathe. A skew chisel will enable you to preserve the rounded end of the piece. Holding the tool with an underhanded grip and bracing the handle against your hip, make a series of V-cuts with the long point of the blade until the piece breaks off. Since the workpiece is thin, support it lightly with your free hand as you turn it, keeping your fingers well clear of the tool rest *(above)*. Once the piece is off the lathe, sand the top smooth. To finish the job, weight the bottom of the chessmen; this will prevent the top-heavy pieces from toppling. Drill a shallow hole in the bottom of the pieces and melt in some solder; non-flux solder with 50 percent lead works best. Once the solder hardens, cover each hole with a felt base. Adhesive-backed felt is available in most hardware stores as pre-punched disks or in sheets that can be trimmed to size.

SHOP TIP

A layout tool for multiple turnings

A chess set requires 32 pieces; transferring layout lines to each workpiece can be time-consuming. A series of jigs like the one shown at right enables you to do the job quickly and accurately. Trace your design onto a piece of scrap and drive a finishing nail into the edge at each transition point. Snip off the nail heads and file the ends to sharp points. Simply press the jig against the spinning blank; the nails will score all the layout lines on the blank at once.

PREPARING THE CASTLE

1 Drilling the hole in the top
The castle is one of the chessmen that needs some additional work after you finish with it on the lathe. Cut the top flat, then fit your drill press with a bit of the same diameter as the top of the castle, less ⅛ inch. To hold the piece steady on the machine table, cut small notches in the jaws of a handscrew and secure the piece in the notches. Center the castle under the bit, clamp the handscrew to the table, and bore the hole to about the first bead on the piece *(right)*.

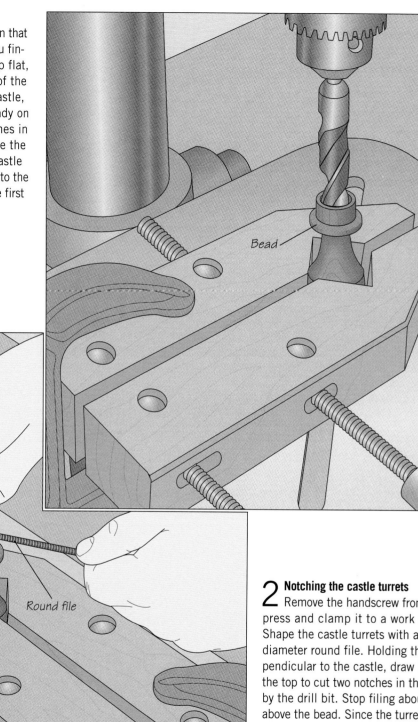

Bead

Round file

2 Notching the castle turrets
Remove the handscrew from the drill press and clamp it to a work surface. Shape the castle turrets with an ⅛-inch-diameter round file. Holding the file perpendicular to the castle, draw it across the top to cut two notches in the walls left by the drill bit. Stop filing about ⅛ inch above the bead. Since the turret walls are thin, use light pressure, particularly when filing the second set of notches *(left)*. Locate the second set 90° away from the first. Use the same file to cut the notches in the King and Queen's crowns.

CRIBBAGE BOARD

The first step in making a cribbage board is to determine its final dimensions based on the number of holes you plan to drill. Typically, cribbage boards feature a starting line of four holes and four rows of 30 holes each. The pattern shown in the photograph at right and in the illustration below also includes a center row with 20 holes to tally up the number of games won. A 4-by-12-inch board will give you enough room to space the holes properly. If you intend to turn the pegs *(page 107)*, plan on drilling ⅛-inch-diameter holes. Pins thinner than this will be difficult to produce.

Molding the ends and edges of a cribbage board adds visual interest to a simple, classic design. The board shown above was made from a piece of purpleheart; the pegs were turned from birch dowel stock.

MAKING THE BOARD

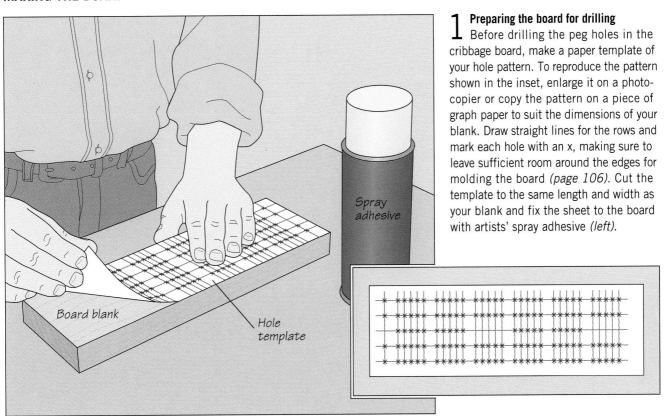

Board blank

Spray adhesive

Hole template

1 Preparing the board for drilling
Before drilling the peg holes in the cribbage board, make a paper template of your hole pattern. To reproduce the pattern shown in the inset, enlarge it on a photocopier or copy the pattern on a piece of graph paper to suit the dimensions of your blank. Draw straight lines for the rows and mark each hole with an x, making sure to leave sufficient room around the edges for molding the board *(page 106)*. Cut the template to the same length and width as your blank and fix the sheet to the board with artists' spray adhesive *(left)*.

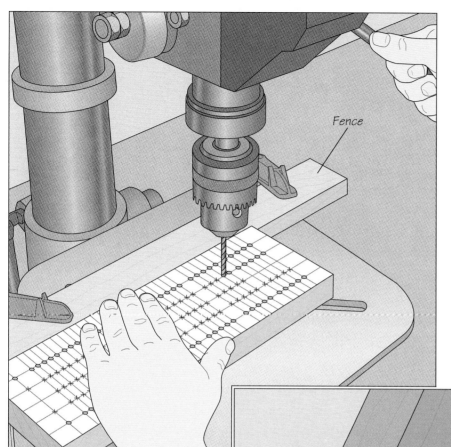

2 Drilling the holes

Set the blank on your drill press table, align one of the outside rows under the bit, and clamp a board to the table flush against the workpiece. The board will serve as a fence, helping you keep the holes in each row perfectly aligned. Set the drilling depth at one-half the board thickness and bore the holes, keeping the workpiece flush against the fence. Once the first row is finished, turn the board around and drill the other outside row of holes. Reposition the fence to bore the remaining rows, then continue drilling *(left)*. If boring has caused some tearout on the top surface of the board, joint the face, using a push block to feed the board slowly across the knives set for a very fine cut. Finally, sand the board smooth.

Fence

Featherboard

3 Molding the cribbage board

Install a piloted molding bit in a router, mount the tool in a table, and set a shallow depth of cut. To support the board as you shape its edges, clamp a featherboard to the fence above the bit. Minimize tearout by cutting into the end grain of the board first, shaping the ends before the edges. While running the board past the bit, keep it flush against the fence *(right)*. Once you have shaped all four sides, raise the cutting height, and repeat the process until the desired profile is achieved.

MAKING THE PEGS

1 Turning the pegs

Install a Jacobs chuck on the head-stock of your lathe. Make the cribbage pegs from hardwood dowels, such as birch. For each peg, cut a length of dowel about 1 inch longer than needed. Mount the blank in the chuck and use a small spindle gouge to taper the peg, working from the wide to the narrow end *(right)*. Then fashion a head on the wide end of the peg.

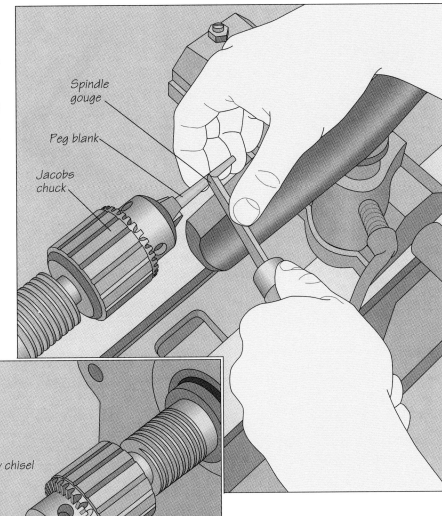

Spindle gouge

Peg blank

Jacobs chuck

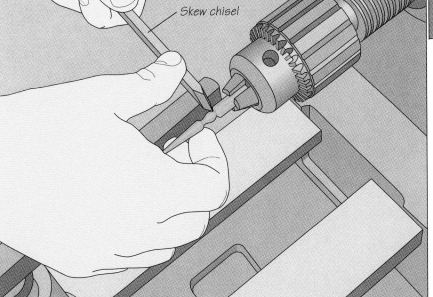

Skew chisel

2 Parting the pegs off

Part the peg off the lathe with a small skew chisel. Cupping your fingers loosely around the peg, make a V-cut just above the top end of the peg's head *(left)*. The peg should drop into your hands.

PUZZLES

Designed and made by Steve Malavolta of Albuquerque, New Mexico, the multi-layered puzzle shown above was assembled from five different woods. From bottom to top, the species are arariba, walnut, bubinga, wenge, and olivewood.

Although making a three-dimensional jigsaw puzzle like the one shown in the photo at left would challenge even the most seasoned woodworker, producing a flat version *(below)* is a relatively simple undertaking. You can select any image for a puzzle: a drawing, postcard, map, or photo. If you do not want to cut up the original, make a color photocopy. In either case, the image should be on a fairly heavy-weight paper. For the base of the puzzle, use hardboard or Baltic birch plywood. Softwood plywoods made from Western fir or Southern pine tend to splinter and require meticulous sanding.

The number of pieces in a puzzle determines its difficulty—both in making it and reassembling it. As shown on page 109, the size of the pieces should be consistent, but you can shape the individual pieces as your skill and creativity dictate. The only requirement is that each piece must contain at least one lobe or socket for each edge.

MAKING A FLAT JIGSAW PUZZLE

1 Mounting the image to the base
Cut the puzzle's base slightly smaller than the image you are using, then bond the paper to the base using a spray adhesive. Flatten down the paper *(right)*, then trim the excess flush with the edges of the base using a sharp utility knife.

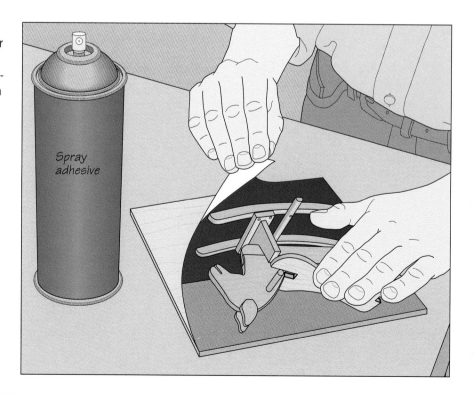

Spray adhesive

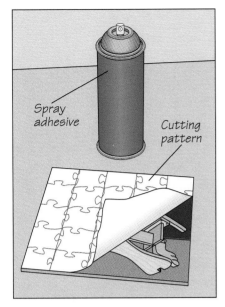

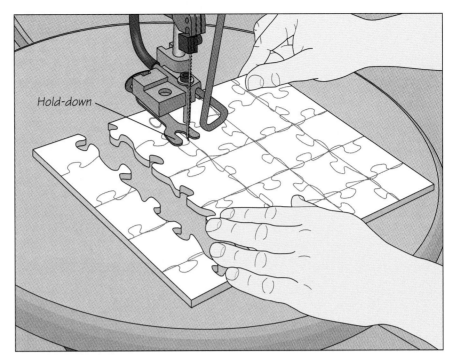

Hold-down

2 Mounting the cutting pattern

As a guide to cutting the puzzle, make a cutting pattern. On a sheet of paper the same size as your image, outline a grid of squares approximating the size of the puzzle pieces, then draw the lobes and sockets of each piece. Use artist's temporary spray adhesive to mount the pattern to the image *(above)*.

3 Cutting the puzzle into strips

Cut out the puzzle on your scroll saw in two steps. To prevent the workpiece from being lifted off the table by the saw's cutting action, install a commercial hold-down on the guide assembly. Start by sawing the workpiece into strips *(above)*, following your cutting pattern. To ensure that the pieces hold together when the puzzle is assembled, flare the tops of the lobes outward.

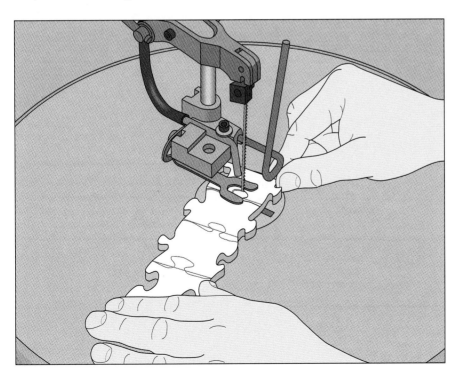

4 Cutting out the pieces

Once the puzzle has been cut into strips, cut out the individual pieces. Feed each strip across the scroll saw table with both hands, making sure your fingers are clear of the blade *(left)*. Make sure the hold-down is pressing the workpiece flat on the table. Once all the pieces are cut, peel off the cutting pattern.

MAKING A BLOCK PUZZLE

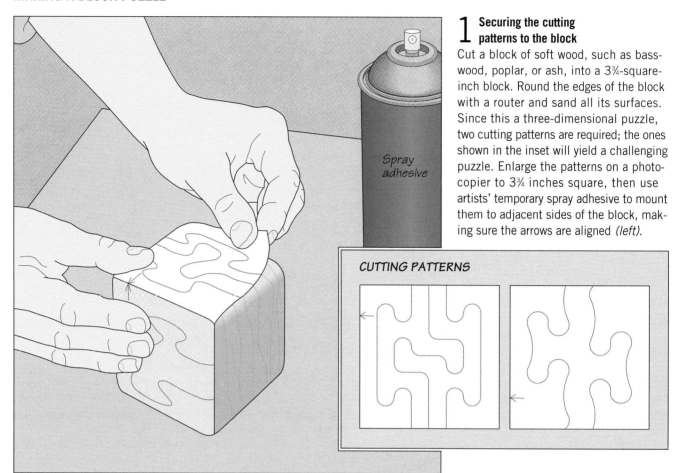

1 Securing the cutting patterns to the block

Cut a block of soft wood, such as basswood, poplar, or ash, into a 3¾-square-inch block. Round the edges of the block with a router and sand all its surfaces. Since this a three-dimensional puzzle, two cutting patterns are required; the ones shown in the inset will yield a challenging puzzle. Enlarge the patterns on a photocopier to 3¾ inches square, then use artists' temporary spray adhesive to mount them to adjacent sides of the block, making sure the arrows are aligned *(left)*.

Spray adhesive

CUTTING PATTERNS

2 Cutting the first face

Install a ⅛-inch-wide hook-tooth blade on your band saw. For best results, change the pulleys on your band saw to produce a slow blade speed of roughly 1200 feet per minute. (For a typical 1725 rpm motor on a 14-inch band saw, you should install a 1½-inch drive pulley on the motor and an 8-inch driven pulley on the saw.) Set the block on the saw table so that one of the cutting patterns is facing up. Aligning the blade with one of the cutting marks, feed the block slowly into the blade with both hands *(right)*. A slow feed rate will prevent the blade from bowing, which would produce an irregular kerf and prevent the puzzle from sliding apart.

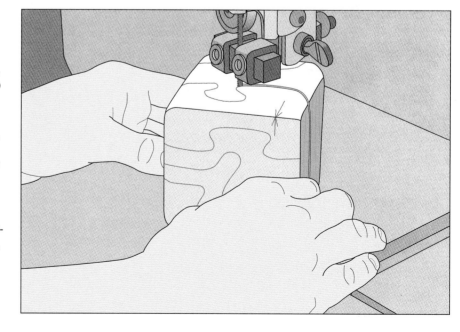

3 **Reassembling the block**
Before you can cut the adjacent face of the block, you need to put it back together. Use two strips of strong masking tape, making sure all four sides of the block are flat and perfectly aligned *(right)*.

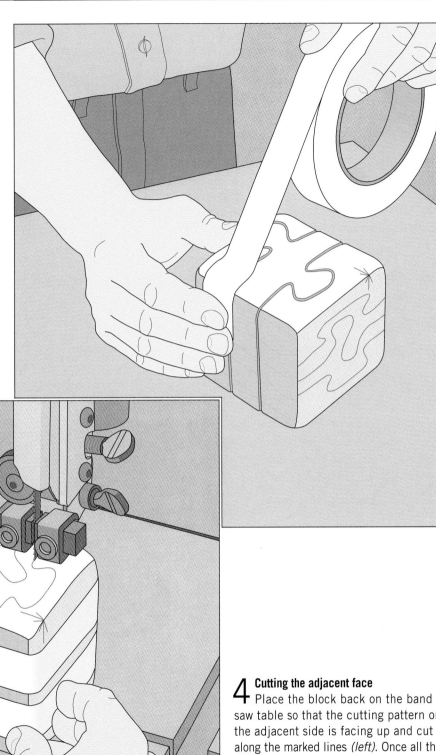

4 **Cutting the adjacent face**
Place the block back on the band saw table so that the cutting pattern on the adjacent side is facing up and cut along the marked lines *(left)*. Once all the cuts are made, remove the cutting patterns and the tape from the block. If the puzzle does not slide apart easily, sand the saw kerfs with a piece of sandpaper wrapped around a dowel.

NATURAL WOOD JIGSAW PUZZLE

MAKING AN ALL-WOOD JIGSAW PUZZLE

1 Cutting out the main elements

The method shown here and on page 113 allows you to create three puzzles with the same basic design, but with different colors and cutting patterns. Plane three boards to a thickness of ¼ inch and trim them to the same length and width. Aligning the edges and ends of the boards, bond them together temporarily with dabs of epoxy glue at the corners. Then draw your design directly on the top piece with a pencil, starting with a ¼- to ½-inch border on all sides. The design should have the same number of elements as layers—in this case, mountains, sun, and sky. This enables you to mix and match the elements, creating three differently colored puzzles. Install a fine blade in your scroll saw; a 0.016-inch-thick and 0.043-inch-wide blade will work well. Using a hold-down to keep the workpiece from lifting off the saw table, cut along the marked lines separating the main elements *(right)*. Feed slowly to prevent the blade from bowing; the three layers must be identical. Leave the border line intact.

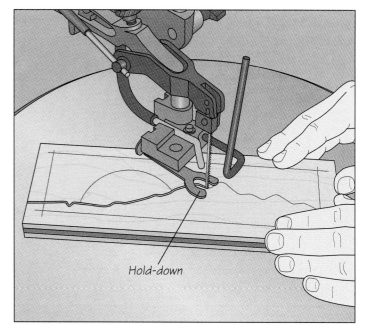

Hold-down

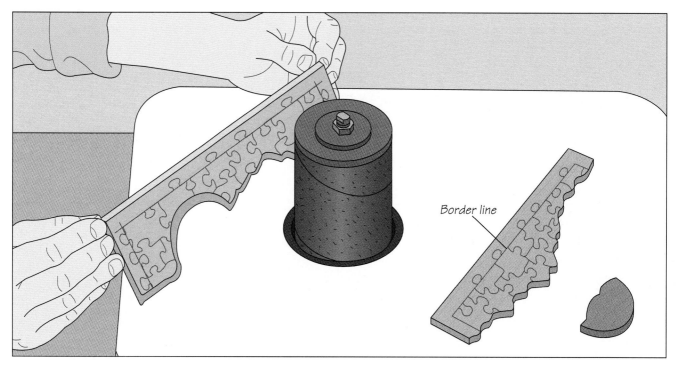

Border line

2 Sanding the elements

Separate the three layers with a utility knife, then combine the nine pieces into three mountain-sun-sky groups, mixing up the colors. Working on each group individually, mark your cutting pattern directly on the wood. Each piece should have at least 3 or 4 lobes or sockets; extend the pattern across the border line so the frame will be part of the puzzle. Then, to give the puzzle the illusion of depth, use a spindle sander to bevel the mating edges of the puzzle. Avoid sanding off too much wood or you will end up with noticeable gaps between the pieces.

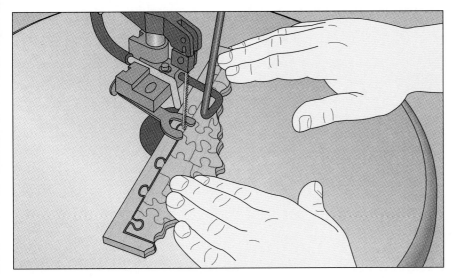

3 Cutting out the frame pieces
Once the bevels have been sanded, cut out the the frame pieces on the scroll saw. With the hold-down in position, cut along the border line and the lobe and socket marks *(left)*, feeding the workpiece with both hands.

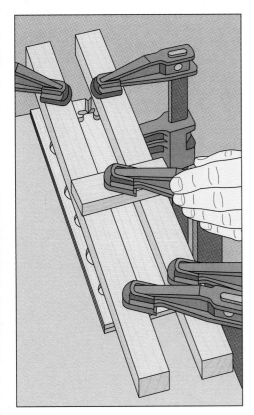

4 Mounting the frame pieces to a base
Cut a wood base to the same size as your puzzle, then spread some glue on the underside of the frame pieces and position them on the base. To secure the pieces while the adhesive cures, lay a grid of clamping blocks across the assembly to distribute the pressure and clamp down the blocks *(above)*.

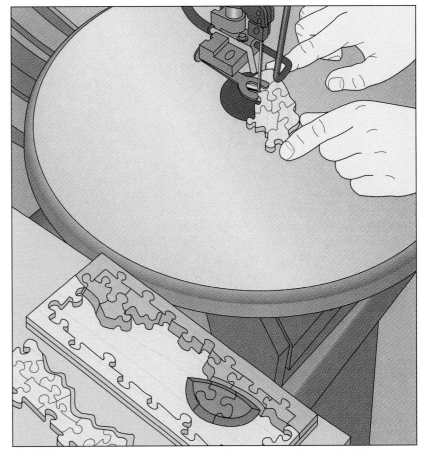

5 Cutting the pieces
If your scroll saw features variable speed, adjust it to about 1000 strokes per minute; if you have a two-speed machine, choose the slow setting. Cut out the individual pieces of the puzzle as you would for a flat jigsaw puzzle *(page 109)*. Work slowly, since the pieces will tend to jump as the workpiece becomes smaller.

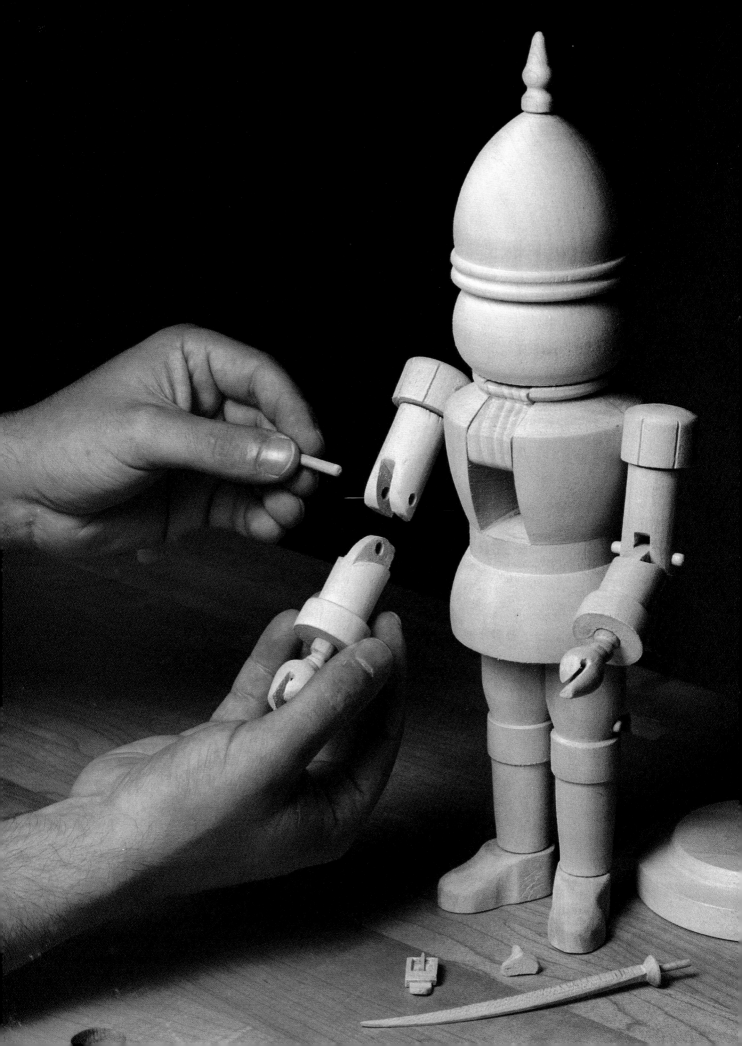

CRAFT CLASSICS

The pau ferro jewelry box shown above conceals a partitioned tray that sits in recesses routed in the sides of the box. The dovetails were produced with a router and a commercial jig, while the finger joints holding the tray together were cut on the table saw.

Whether your goal is to produce a keepsake that will endure as a testament to your woodworking skill or make a gift for a loved one or friend, the projects featured in this chapter will test your abilities and delight the most discriminating audience. The jewelry box shown at right and on page 116, for example, relies on classic joinery techniques to transform a basic container into an attractive and useful treasury. The corners of the box are dovetailed and the tray under the hinged lid is assembled with finger joints. A half-mortise lock and an inlay recessed into the top of the lid add the finishing touches. With the same basic techniques and the right dividers or shelves, you can make custom boxes to hold anything from cigars to artists' supplies.

Making a Shaker box, like the one featured starting on page 122, requires a different set of skills. Here, hardwood stock is resawn into 1/16-inch-thick strips, which are moistened in hot water and bent around a wooden core.

The section on making a wooden briefcase *(page 125)* showcases a familiar item in a new light. Using solid wood or veneered plywood, the case is assembled using either miters and splines or box joints; the top pivots on concealed hinges.

The result is a case that is sturdy yet lightweight—and a rare woodworking project that you can carry with you.

The nutcracker shown on page 130 is a fitting project for someone with some basic wood turning experience. The figure consists of more than a dozen small parts, and features articulated joints that enable the nutcracker to strike several lifelike poses, from holding up a flag to brandishing a sword.

While the nutcracker is a relatively time-consuming project, requiring about 20 hours to assemble and finish, the white cedar bird shown on page 136 can be made in a matter of minutes once the technique has been mastered. In fact, the project is designed to be executed quickly, since it involves slicing a wet-wood blank into a series of thin strips. While the wood is green and pliable, the strips can be fanned out into a tail pattern.

The final project in the chapter, the hand mirror, is tailor-made for producing multiple copies. Once you have built the simple jig that allows you to plow out the recess for the mirror, the rest of the job is straightforward work on the band saw and the router table. As shown on page 139 you can give each mirror a one-of-a-kind appeal by laminating contrasting wood species and creating unique patterns for the blank.

Based on a design by Fred Sneath of Stony Lake, Ontario, the nutcracker at left features articulated joints that allow the wrists, elbows, and shoulders of the figure to move. The nutcracking jaw/crank, which runs vertically up through the torso, pivots on a metal rod. As shown on page 130, Sneath's nutcrackers spring to life with the combination of finishes he uses—a base coat of urethane covered by artists' acrylics for the colored parts and brush-on lacquer for the metallic accents.

JEWELRY BOX

A jewelry box should do more than keep the dust off valuables. It should also suggest strength and security—and express the elegance of its contents. The box shown in the photo at left satisfies these requirements in a number of ways. It is made from an exotic hardwood—

Made from pau ferro, the jewelry box shown above measures 9 ½ inches long by 6 ¼ inches deep and 5 ½ inches high. The box sits in a rabbeted base joined at the corners by miters.

pau ferro—and is joined at the corners by through dovetails, a sturdy joint that adds visual interest. The half-mortise lock protects the contents from prying fingers and accents the design of the piece. The tray inside the box features dividers for sorting smaller items and is assembled with finger joints.

For a box of the proportions shown, use ½- to ⅜-inch-thick stock for the the box and ¼-inch-thick wood for the tray. To protect the jewelry from scratches, you can line the inside of the box and tray with a soft material such as felt or flocking (*page 129*).

MAKING THE BOX

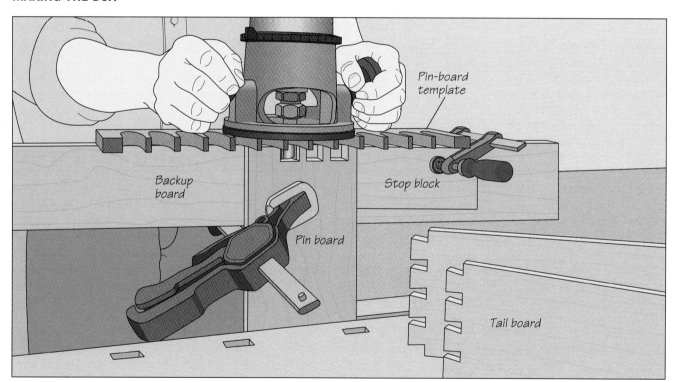

Pin-board template

Backup board

Stop block

Pin board

Tail board

1 Routing the dovetails

To cut the dovetails for the box with a router and the jig shown above, screw the pin- and tail-board templates to backup boards, then secure one of the tail boards (the sides of the box) end up in a bench vise. Clamp the tail template to the workpiece so the underside of the template is butted against the end of the board. Also clamp a stop block against one edge of the workpiece so the tails at the other end and in the other tail board will match. Install a top-piloted dovetail bit in the router and cut the tails by feeding the tool along the top of the template and moving the bit in and out of the jig's slots. Keep the bit pilot pressed against the sides of the slots throughout. Repeat to rout the tails at the other end of the board, and in the other tail board. Then use the completed tails to outline the pins on the front and back of the box. Secure the pin board in the vise, clamp the pin template to the board with the slots aligned over the outline, and secure a stop block in place. Rout the pins with a straight bit (*above*).

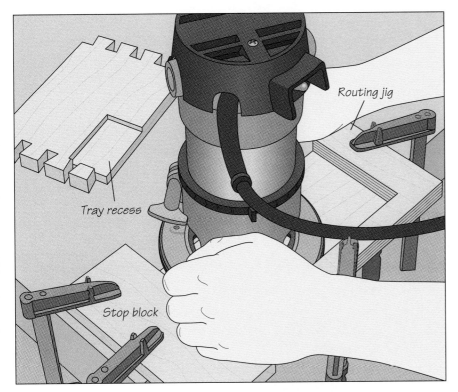

Tray recess

Routing jig

Stop block

2 Routing the recesses for the tray

The tray inside the box rests in a recess routed into both sides of the box. Before cutting the recesses, dry-assemble the box and determine what should be the top of the box depending on the grain and figure of the wood. Label the pieces to facilitate reassembly, then outline the recesses on the sides and set one of the pieces inside-face up on a work surface. You can make a simple jig to keep the router bit within the outline by cutting a notch out of a piece of plywood and clamping it to the workpiece. Also clamp a stop block along the tails to prevent from cutting into them. Install a straight bit in the router, set the cutting depth to ¼ inch and rout the recess. Repeat for the other side *(left)*, then square the corners with a chisel.

3 Preparing the box for the bottom

The bottom of the jewelery box fits into a rabbet along the inside of the box. Dry-fit the parts together, then clamp the unit securely, installing the jaws on the sides of the box. Fit a router with a piloted rabbeting bit of a diameter equal to one-half the thickness of the stock. Then mount the router in a table and set the cutting height to the thickness of the bottom panel you will be using. Set the box right-side up on the table and, starting at the middle of one side, feed the stock into the bit against the direction of bit rotation. Keeping the pilot bearing butted against the workpiece, feed the box clockwise *(right)*. Continue pivoting the box on the table until you return to your starting point. Use veneered plywood for the bottom and cut the panel to fit the opening. The plywood will not expand or contract with changes in humidity, allowing you to glue and nail it in place.

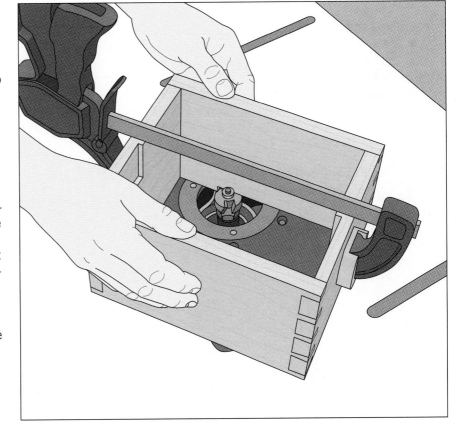

INSTALLING THE LOCK

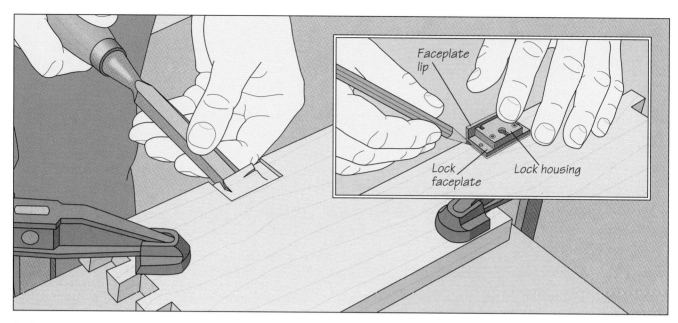

Cutting the lock mortise

Lay the front of the box inside-face up and position the lock face-down midway between the pins and flush with the top edge of the board. Trace the outline of the hardware *(inset)*, then extend the lines onto the top edge of the board. Now clamp the front of the box to your work surface and use a chisel to cut a shallow mortise for the faceplate lip in the top edge of the board. Score the mortise outline on the inside face of the board then, holding the chisel horizontally and bevel up, shave away the waste in thin layers *(above)*. The central portion of the mortise, which will hold the lock housing, must be deeper than the portion housing the faceplate. Periodically test-fit the lock in the cavity and use the chisel to deepen or widen the mortise as necessary. Once the faceplate is flush with the inside face of the board, set the lock in the mortise and mark the location of the keyhole. (The mortise for the lock can also be cut out with a router, but work carefully, especially if you are doing the job freehand. Do not try to rout right to the edge of the mortise outline; instead, finish the cut with a chisel.) Now drill a hole for the key through the board and use a small, round file to refine the opening to the shape of the key, then install the escutcheon over the keyhole and screw the lock to the front of the box. You can now glue up the box.

MAKING THE BASE MOLDING

1 Shaping the molding stock

Because the pieces for the base molding are relatively narrow, shape both edges of a wide board, then rip the molding from the board. Install a molding bit in a router and mount the tool in a table. To prevent kickback, use three featherboards, clamping one to the table in line with the bit and two to the fence, one on each side of the cutter. (The featherboard on the outfeed side of the fence has been removed for clarity.) Shape both edges of the board, feeding it along the fence *(right)*.

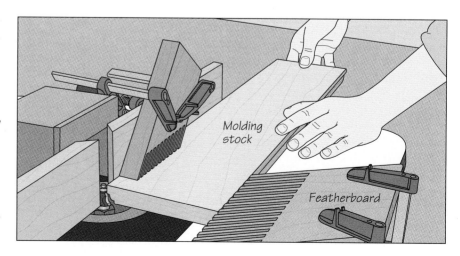

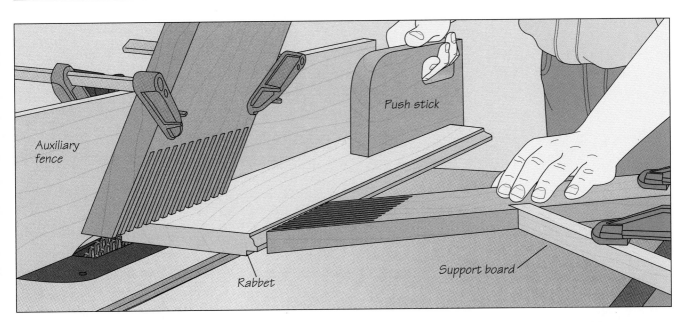

Auxiliary
fence

Push stick

Rabbet

Support board

2 Preparing the molding for the box

Cut rabbets in the molding by fitting your table saw with a dado head. Adjust the width of the head to two-thirds the thickness of the stock and the cutting height to one-third the stock thickness. Fasten an auxiliary fence to the rip fence and notch it with the dado head. Use two featherboards to support the stock, clamping one to the fence above the blade and one to the table; brace the second featherboard with a support board. Feed the stock along the fence to cut a rabbet on one edge, then repeat on the other edge, making both passes with a push stick *(above)*. Now rip the molding pieces from the board. If you wish, you can use a band saw to cut a relief pattern in the molding like the one shown in the photo on page 116, creating feet at each corner.

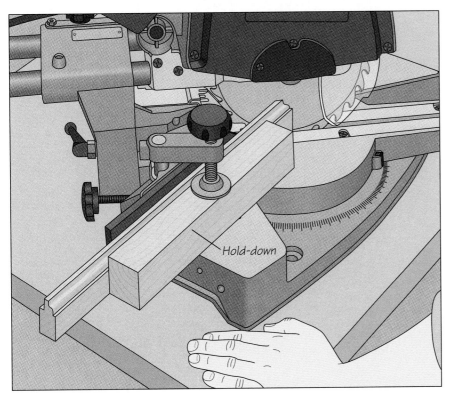

Hold-down

3 Mitering and installing the molding

You can saw the molding pieces to length with a miter box or on a power miter saw adjusted for a 45° cut. Lay the stock on edge against the fence, butt a board against the workpiece, and clamp it in place as a hold-down. To ensure the molding fits the box perfectly, make the first cuts a little long, test-fit the molding under the box, and trim the pieces to fit *(left)*. Spread glue on the mitered ends of the molding and secure the pieces together with a web clamp, using the box as a form. Once the glue has cured, apply adhesive in the rabbets and set the box on the molding.

MOUNTING THE LID

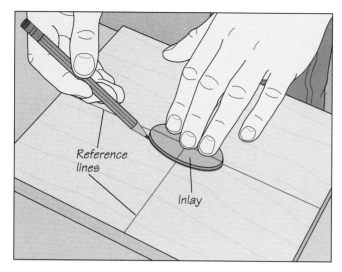

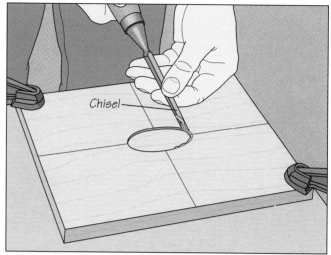

1 Installing the inlay

Mark two lines across the lid of the box that intersect at its center. Mark corresponding lines that cross at the center of the inlay, then position the inlay on the top so the four reference marks line up and trace the outline with a pencil *(above, left)*. Clamp the top to a work surface and use a router fitted with a straight bit to cut the recess to within $\frac{1}{16}$ inch of your outline; the depth of the recess should equal the inlay thickness. To complete the recess, score the outline with a utility knife and cut to the marked outline with a chisel *(above, right)*. Then spread a thin coating of glue in the recess, set the inlay in place, and clamp it down using a wood block to distribute the pressure. Once the glue has cured, sand the inlay flush with the surface. Now install a piloted round-over bit in a router and bullnose the edges of the top by making a pass on each side, making sure you keep the bearing butted against the stock while you feed against the direction of bit rotation.

2 Installing the lid hinges

Attach the hinges to the jewelry box in two steps. Start by outlining one leaf of each hinge on the lid, then cut mortises within the outlines and fasten the hinges to the lid. Make the mortises $\frac{1}{32}$ inch deeper than the leaf thickness. Next, position the lid on the box and outline the remaining leaves on the top edge of the back of the box. Clamp the box to a work surface and use a chisel to cut the mortises *(right)*.

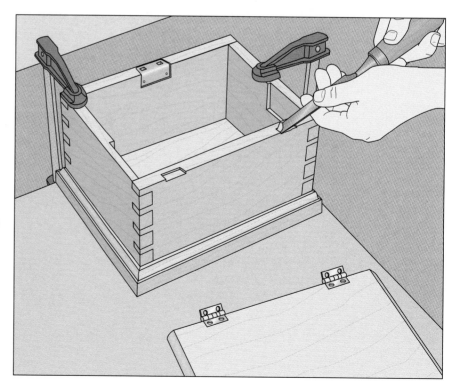

3 Installing the lid and the lock strike plate

Before fastening the hinges to the box, mount the strike plate to the underside of the lid. Position the plate on the lock and turn the key to hold the plate in place. Apply double-sided tape to the strike plate and position the lid on the box. Turn the key again to release the strike plate and remove the lid; the plate will be in position on the lid. Outline the strike plate on the surface, remove the tape, and cut a mortise within the outline to the depth of the plate. Then drill pilot holes and screw the plate in place (right). To complete the lid installation, screw the hinges to the box.

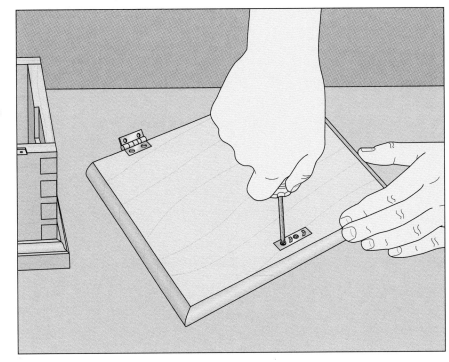

INSTALLING THE TRAY

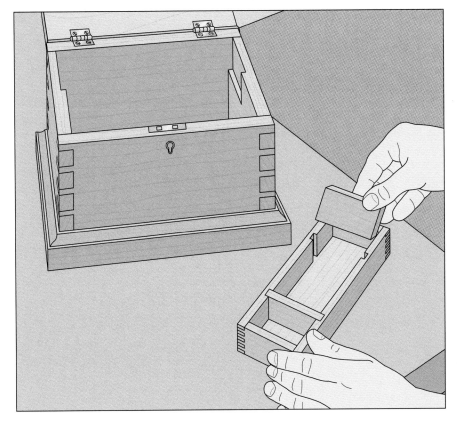

Making the tray

Cut the sides of the tray to fit in the recess in the box and join the pieces with box joints (page 125). Before assembling the tray, cut dadoes for the dividers in the inside faces of the front and back. Glue up the tray, cut and insert the dividers (left), and set the tray in the box. Sand the tray as necessary to fine-tune its fit. As a final touch, you can attach a chain to the lid and box to prevent the lid from opening too far and straining the hinges.

SHAKER BOX

First produced in the 1790s, Shaker boxes were made in graduated sizes to hold household goods; when empty they could be nested inside one another. The smallest size, 000, is a 1 inch-by-2-inch ellipse; the largest box, number 20, made from two bands more than 9 feet long, is 26 inches by 38½ inches.

The oval boxes remain popular today, and can be easily made from commercial kits, which sell the bands already cut to the proper thickness and size and the templates needed to trace the distinctive "swallowtail" fingers. You may choose to cut the bands yourself from a hardwood such as cherry or maple.

Made from quartersawn cherry veneers, the round Shaker boxes shown at left are soaked in boiling water until they are soft enough to be bent around a form. Once the joint is marked on the edge, the sheets are then clinched with copper tacks and allowed to dry.

BENDING A SHAKER BOX

1 Cutting the fingers
To make a Shaker box from a commercial kit, first prepare the stock for the two bands—one for the box and one for the top. The bands are typically resawn from hardwood stock to a thickness of ¹⁄₁₆ inch. For best results, use straight-grained, quartersawn stock that has been air dried to a moisture content of 15 to 20 percent. Use the proper-sized finger template to outline the fingers on the box band *(right)* then mark the tack holes and drill them with a ¹⁄₁₆-inch bit. Repeat for the top band.

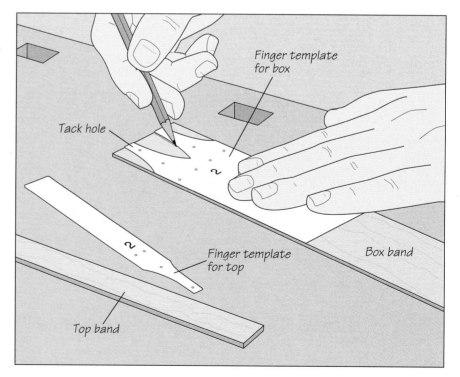

Finger template for box

Tack hole

Finger template for top

Box band

Top band

2 Beveling the fingers

Clamp the bands to a backup board and bevel the fingers with a utility knife. Holding the knife firmly with both hands, cut an angle of 10° around the fingers *(right)*. Then taper the outside face of the opposite end of each band using a belt sander, starting with the taper about 1½ inches in from the end. This will ensure a smooth overlap and uniform thickness once the bands are bent.

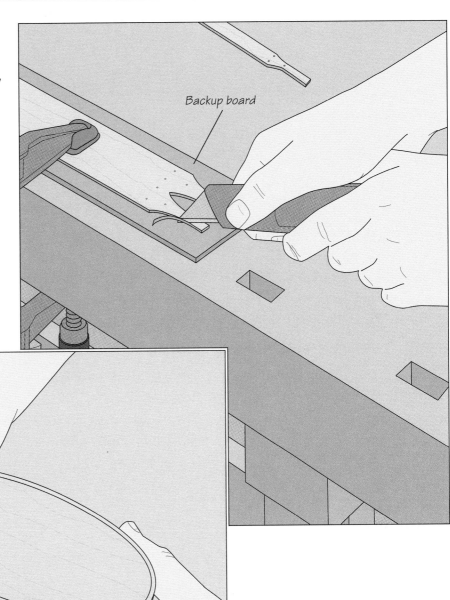

Backup board

3 Marking the joint

Soak the box and lid bands in boiling water until they are soft—typically about 20 minutes. Remove the box band from the water and wrap it around the proper-sized box core so the beveled fingers lap over the tapered end. Make a reference mark across the edges of the band where the ends overlap *(left)*. Keep the beveled fingers pressed tightly against the core to prevent them from splitting.

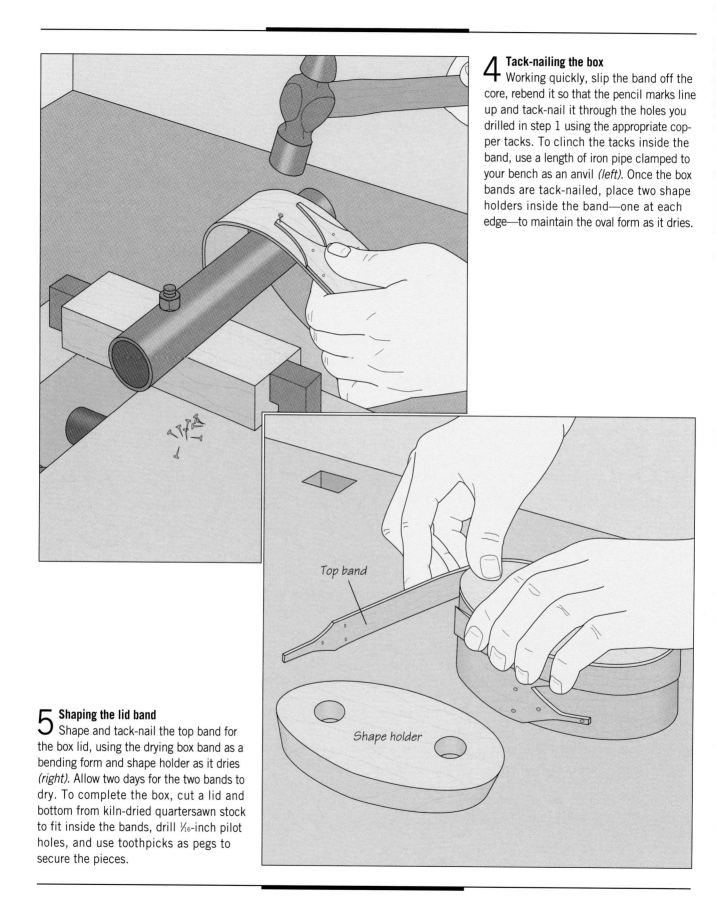

4 Tack-nailing the box

Working quickly, slip the band off the core, rebend it so that the pencil marks line up and tack-nail it through the holes you drilled in step 1 using the appropriate copper tacks. To clinch the tacks inside the band, use a length of iron pipe clamped to your bench as an anvil *(left)*. Once the box bands are tack-nailed, place two shape holders inside the band—one at each edge—to maintain the oval form as it dries.

Top band

Shape holder

5 Shaping the lid band

Shape and tack-nail the top band for the box lid, using the drying box band as a bending form and shape holder as it dries *(right)*. Allow two days for the two bands to dry. To complete the box, cut a lid and bottom from kiln-dried quartersawn stock to fit inside the bands, drill 1⁄16-inch pilot holes, and use toothpicks as pegs to secure the pieces.

BRIEFCASE

A wooden briefcase should have all the features of any well-made briefcase: clean, attractive lines and lightweight strength. With a material such as wood, this can present a challenge, since strength and lightness are an uncommon combination. When sizing your stock, make the briefcase frame as thin as possible without sacrificing solidity. If you are using walnut or cherry, the stock should be at least ½ inch thick. The side panels of the briefcase should also be sturdy, since they help hold the unit together and keep the frame square. A good choice is ¼-inch hardwood plywood. The side panels of the case shown in the photo at right are made of solid white cedar boards edge-glued togeth-

er. Solid-wood sides are more attractive than plywood, but not as rigid—and solid wood may present problems due to wood movement.

The design described in this section uses concealed Soss-type hinges and a laminated handle. The inside of the case can be lined with leather or, as shown on page 129, flocked with artificial suede.

Made from cherry and white cedar, the briefcase shown at right features corners that are joined by miter-and-spline joints. The finger-joint method described below will produce an equally sturdy case.

MAKING THE BRIEFCASE FRAME

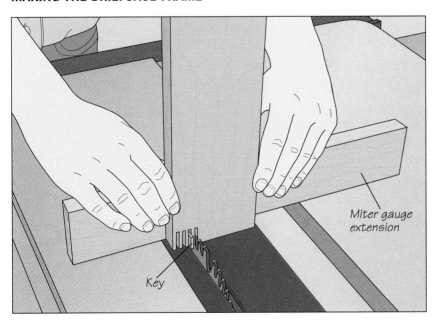

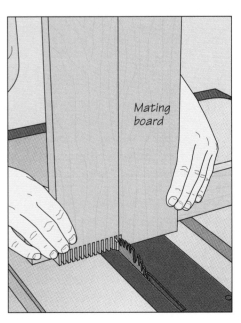

1 Cutting the finger joints

You can cut the notches for finger joints one after another on your table saw with a simple jig made from an extension board fastened to the miter gauge. Set the cutting height of the blade to the stock thickness, clamp the extension to the miter gauge, and feed it into the blade to cut a notch. Slide the extension along the gauge so the gap between the notch and the blade is equal to the notch width, then screw the extension to the gauge. Cut a second notch, then insert a wooden key in the first notch so it projects at least 1 inch from the extension.

Butt the edge of one of the frame pieces against the key, hold its face against the extension and cut a notch. Then fit the notch over the key and make a second cut. Continue cutting notches in this manner *(above, left)* until you reach the opposite side of the workpiece. To cut the remaining fingers, turn the workpiece around and fit the first notch you cut over the key. Butt one edge of the mating board against the first board, and feed it into the blade *(above, right)*. Continue cutting notches in the board following the same procedure you used on the first one.

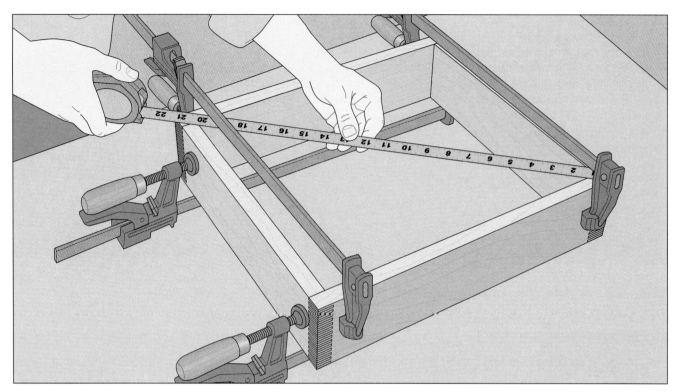

2 Gluing up the frame

Use a small nail to spread glue in between the fingers in the frame pieces, applying as even a coat as possible. Fit the boards together and secure the joints with four bar clamps, aligning a clamp with each side of the frame just inside the fingers. To check the frame for square, measure the diagonals between opposite corners *(above)*. The two results should be the same. If not, install another clamp across the longer of the two diagonals, setting the clamp jaws on those already in place. Tighten the clamps a little at a time, measuring as you go until the two diagonals are equal.

3 Ripping the frame in two

Divide the frame into two parts—the main body and the top—on your table saw. Fasten a 6- to 8-inch-wide auxiliary fence to the rip fence and adjust the cutting width to one-third to one-quarter the height of the frame, ensuring that the blade aligns with one of the fingers of the corner joint. Set the cutting height slightly above the thickness of the stock. Feed the frame into the blade with both hands, keeping it flush against the fence *(right)*.

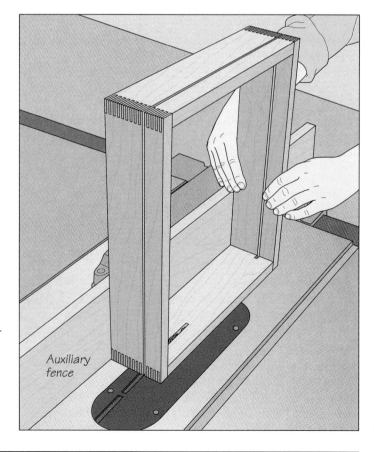

Auxiliary fence

4 Preparing the frame for the hinges
The hinges that will connect the lid and body of the frame together fit into holes in the edges of the stock. Clamp an auxiliary plywood table to your drill press table and install a bit equal to the hinge diameter. Set the cutting depth equal to the length of the hinge cylinder, adding $\frac{3}{16}$ inch to allow for the rabbet you will cut around the frame in step 5. Holding the lid on the table, bore the holes into the edge of the bottom about 3 inches from each end *(right)*. Repeat on the body.

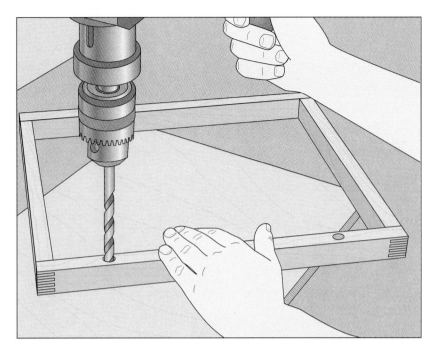

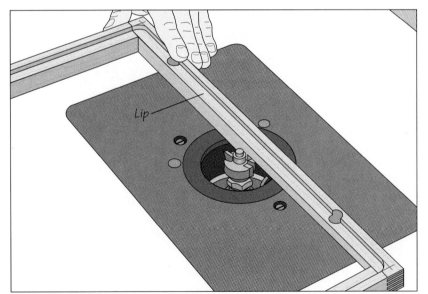

5 Preparing the lid and body for assembly
Install a rabbeting bit in a router and mount the tool in a table. Start by routing a rabbet around the inside edges of the lid. Make the depth of the cut $\frac{1}{8}$ inch, with a width equal to one-half the stock thickness; the resulting lip will mate with a rabbet in the body *(step 7)*, allowing the pieces to interlock when the case is closed. Next, you need to rout rabbets along the outside edges of the lid and body to accommodate the side panels of the briefcase. Raise the cutting height to the side panel thickness and set the lid outside-face down on the router table. Pressing the stock against the bit pilot, feed the lid in a clockwise direction *(above)* until the rabbet is cut all around the perimeter. Repeat on the outside edges of the body.

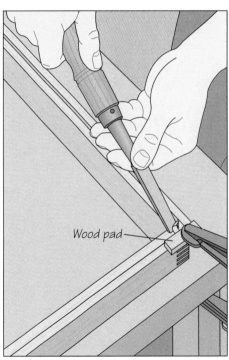

6 Squaring the corners of the rabbets
The router will leave rabbets with rounded corners. To square the corners, clamp the lid to a work surface, protecting the stock with a wood pad, and use a chisel to remove the waste *(above)*. Repeat to square the rabbet corners on the body.

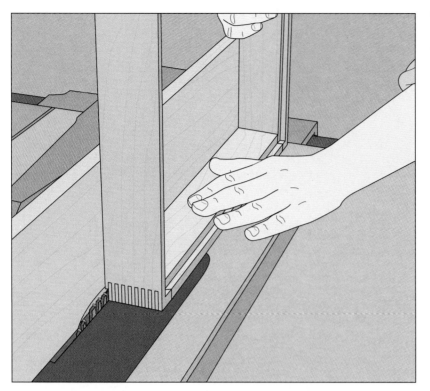

7 Preparing the body for the lid

Cut the rabbets to mate with the lid around the inside edge of the body on your table saw. Leaving the auxiliary fence you used in step 3 on the rip fence, set the cutting height so the rabbet you cut will mate with the one in the lid; one-half the stock thickness should be about right. Holding the inside edge of the body against the fence, feed it into the blade *(left)*. Repeat the cut on the remaining three sides.

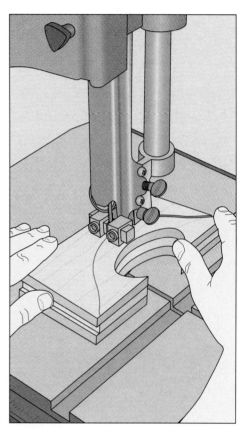

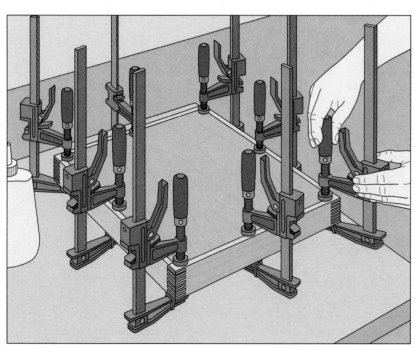

8 Installing the side panels

Cut the side panels of the briefcase to fit in the rabbets along the outside edges of the lid and body. Spread glue in the rabbets, set the panel in place, and install clamps around the perimeter of the piece at 6-inch intervals to secure the panel in place as the adhesive cures *(above)*.

9 Making the handle

Make the briefcase handle by face-gluing three pieces of ¼-inch-thick wood together. For added strength, alternate the grain direction of the boards. Outline the shape of the handle on the top piece and cut it out on your band saw *(above)*. Then round over the top edge of the handle on a table-mounted router and finish shaping it to fit your hand with a spindle sander. Attach the handle to the case with glue and screws drilled and countersunk from inside the case.

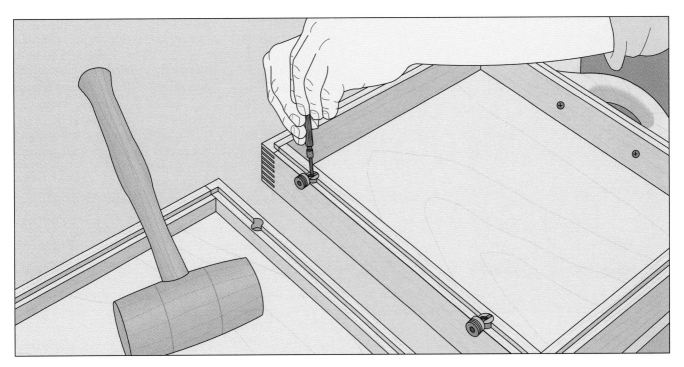

10 Installing the hinges

The hinges shown above have a small setscrew that makes the cylinder expand when tightened. Loosen the setscrews, then push the hinge cylinders into their holes in the case body. The cylinders should be flush with the bottom of the rabbet.

Tighten the setscrews to secure the hardware in place *(above)*. Line the interior of the case *(step 11)*, if desired, then insert the hinges into the lid and tighten the hinge screws to complete the installation.

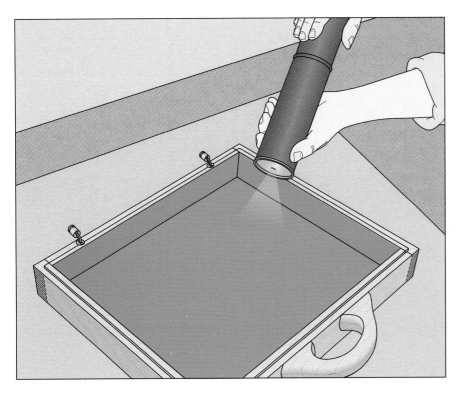

11 Flocking the interior

Flocking is a simple, inexpensive way to impart a suede-like feel to almost any surface, such as the inside of the briefcase or a jewelry box. Kits are available from most woodworking suppliers. Start by coating the surface with the adhesive provided, then, holding the flocking gun 8 to 10 inches from case at an angle betwen 45° and 90°, pump on the fibers. Let the adhesive dry for about 10 hours and remove any excess fiber, which can be reused for other projects. To complete the briefcase, screw a pair of draw catches to the main body and top to keep the case closed.

NUTCRACKER

Shaping and assembling the many parts of the nutcrackers shown in this section may be time-consuming, but with a methodical approach, the process is not difficult. And as the photo at left shows, the results are well worth the trouble.

Most of the parts are produced on the lathe; in fact, all the major components—the torso and head, the arms and the legs—are turned from only three blanks, which makes assembly simpler and more precise. Sawing all the arm parts from a single spindle turning, for example, helps ensure that the arms will be of uniform size and that the elbow joints will fit together well. Once the major parts are done, the hands, feet, and nose can be carved to fit and individualize the figure.

Choose a soft, easy-to-shape wood like basswood for the main components of the nutcracker. Ash is a good choice for the jaw/crank; the wrists are best made from standard birch doweling.

Distinctive coloring and attention to detail breathe life into the nutcrackers shown at left, built by Fred Sneath of Stony Lake, Ontario. Although the main parts of the figures—the torso, arms and legs—are virtually identical, the nutcrackers are given unique personalities with different paints, helmets, and facial features. The beard and hair can be made from imitation fur, yarn, or carpeting.

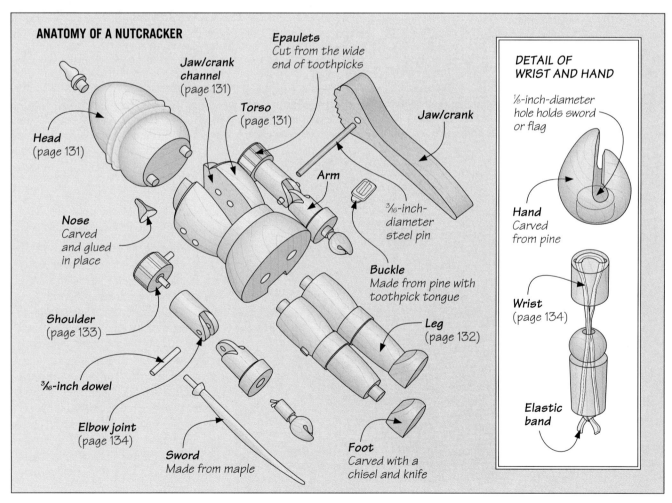

ANATOMY OF A NUTCRACKER

Head
(page 131)

Jaw/crank channel
(page 131)

Epaulets
Cut from the wide end of toothpicks

Torso
(page 131)

Jaw/crank

Arm

Nose
Carved and glued in place

³⁄₁₆-inch-diameter steel pin

Buckle
Made from pine with toothpick tongue

Shoulder
(page 133)

Leg
(page 132)

³⁄₁₆-inch dowel

Elbow joint
(page 134)

Sword
Made from maple

Foot
Carved with a chisel and knife

DETAIL OF WRIST AND HAND

⅛-inch-diameter hole holds sword or flag

Hand
Carved from pine

Wrist
(page 134)

Elastic band

MAKING A NUTCRACKER

1 Turning the head and torso

Cut a blank that is long enough for the head and torso and mount it between centers on your lathe. Use a spindle gouge and a skew chisel to turn the blank to the shape shown at right, making the diameters at the shoulders and hips about equal. Once the turning is done, leave the blank spinning on the machine and use a piece of sandpaper to smooth the surface, bringing the abrasive up to the stock from below. Make sure the lines defining the belt remain distinct. Then cut the head from the torso on a band saw.

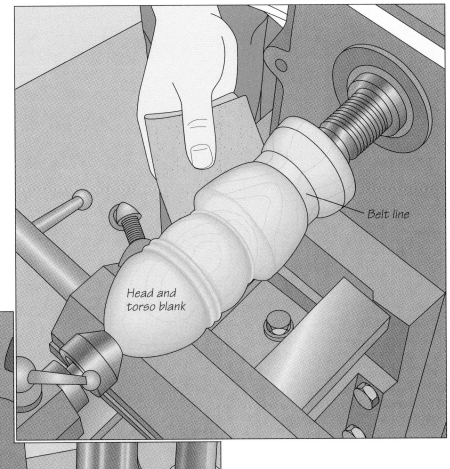

Belt line

Head and
torso blank

2 Cutting out the channel for the jaw/crank

Cut the channel in the torso for the jaw/crank in two steps, starting on the band saw. Outline a ¾-inch-wide channel in the middle of the torso from the top to the belt line, then secure the piece in a handscrew so the outline is facing up. Pushing the clamp to feed the torso into the blade, cut the sides of the channel, then clear out the waste with a series of angled cuts *(left)*. Square the bottom of the channel with a chisel.

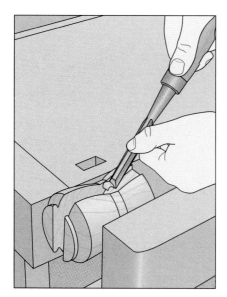

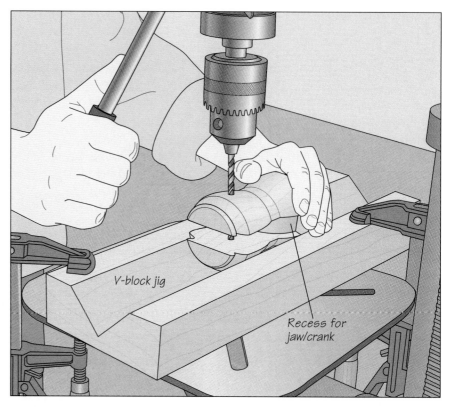

V-block jig

Recess for jaw/crank

3 Angling the jaw/crank channel
Once the channel in the torso is finished, secure the piece back side up in a bench vise and extend the channel along the back of the torso to hold the bottom of the jaw/crank. Holding a chisel at an angle to the piece bevel-side up (above), shave away the waste wood in thin layers to create a slope that angles outward from the middle of the crank mortise to the bottom of the torso. Cut the recess so the top surface of the jaw/crank will be flush with the back of the torso—or protrude only slightly—when it is installed.

4 Drilling the pin and shoulder holes
Referring to the anatomy illustration *(page 130)* for their location, mark the holes for the jaw/crank pin and the shoulders on the torso so the holes will be perpendicular to the channel. Cut a wedge out of a board to make a V-block jig, set the torso in the jig, and place the jig on your drill press table. Install a bit the same diameter as the steel pin, align the marked holes for the pin under the bit, and clamp the jig to the table. Drill the hole for the jaw crank *(above)*, then reposition the torso in the jig and drill the shoulder holes.

5 Turning the legs and arms
Mount a blank between centers on your lathe, ensuring that it is long enough to yield both legs, including the tenons that will join the legs to the torso and feet. Use a roughing gouge to turn the blank into a cylinder, a skew chisel *(right)* and a spindle gouge to add details, and a parting tool to define the tenons. Once the legs are turned, saw them apart. Turn the arms the same way, allowing an extra ½ inch for the overlap at the elbow joint.

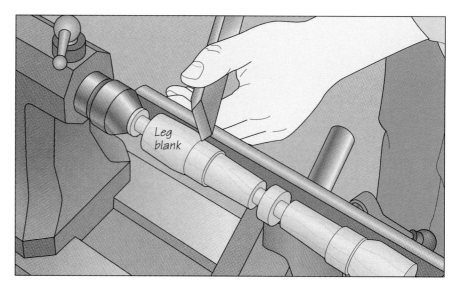

Leg blank

6 Installing the jaw/crank legs and shoulders

Referring to the anatomy illustration on page 130, cut the jaw/crank to shape and fix it in place with the steel pin. Then test-fit the legs against the torso, mark the leg tenons on the torso, and drill the holes to the tenon length. Now glue the legs in place. Carve the feet and drill a hole into each one to accept the tenon at the bottom of the legs. It is easier to drill the dowel holes into the sides of the shoulders before they have been sawn from the arm spindle; secure the arm spindle in a V-block jig *(page 132)* as you bore the holes on the drill press. Now cut the arms into their various sections —upper arms, lower arms, and shoulders—and drill the holes into the bottom of the shoulders for the dowels that will join them to the upper arms. All the holes should be drilled halfway through the stock. Glue the dowels into the shoulder, leaving ⅜ inch of the pins protruding. Wait until the adhesive has cured before fitting the shoulders into the torso *(right)*; otherwise, the glue may bond the joints in place and not allow them to articulate.

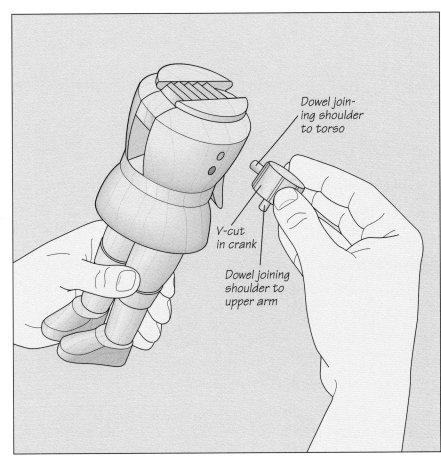

Dowel joining shoulder to torso

V-cut in crank

Dowel joining shoulder to upper arm

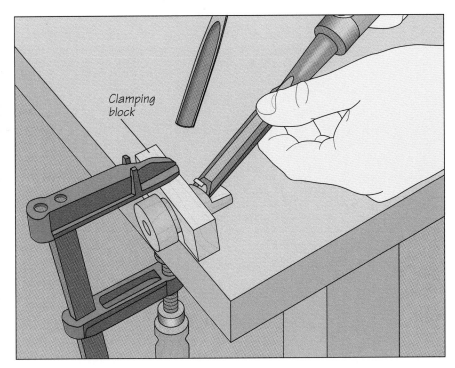

Clamping block

7 Carving the elbow joints

Each elbow joint is an open mortise-and-tenon joint which pivots around a dowel. Cut the tenons in the lower arms and the mortises in the upper arms on your scroll saw. Then clamp one of the lower arms to a work surface, using an arched clamping block to protect the stock. Round over the tenon with a disk sander or gouge and a chisel *(left)*; this will improve the articulating movement of the elbow joint. Repeat with the other lower arm.

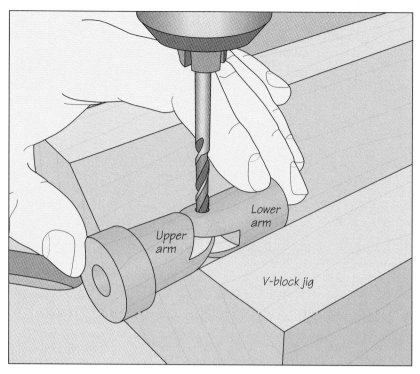

Upper arm

Lower arm

V-block jig

8 Assembling the elbow joint

Fit the lower and upper arms together, then place the assembly in your V-block jig clamped to the drill press table. With one side of the arm facing up, drill right through the mortise and tenon *(above)*. Cut a length of dowel to span the joint and sand the ends smooth, then slip the dowel into the hole. To allow the elbow to move, do not use any glue. You may need to continue rounding over the tenon to perfect the fit, as described in step 7.

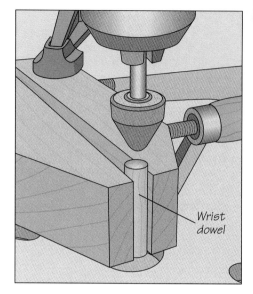

Wrist dowel

9 Preparing the wrist

Refer to the anatomy illustration on page 130 for details of the wrist-to-hand joint. The wrist consists of two lengths of ⅜-inch dowel: one with a ball carved on the top end and another with a matching socket on the bottom. The piece with the socket fits snugly in a hole in the hand. To cut the socket, secure one dowel end-up in a handscrew and fit a rounded grinding stone in a drill press *(above)*. Grind the socket, then carve the matching ball in the other piece.

10 Assembling the wrist

The two parts of the wrist are held together by an elastic band. To prepare the pieces, clamp one in a handscrew and secure the handscrew to a work surface. Then fit an electric drill with a small bit and bore an angled hole that starts at the edge of the flat end and exits in the middle of the ball—or socket—end. Repeat on the other edge *(right)* and for the other part of the wrist. Feed a length of elastic band through the holes to tie the pieces together, using a thin length of wire to help you thread the elastic. Next, carve the hands and drill two holes into each: one into the bottom to accept the wrist and a smaller one to hold a flagpole or sword.

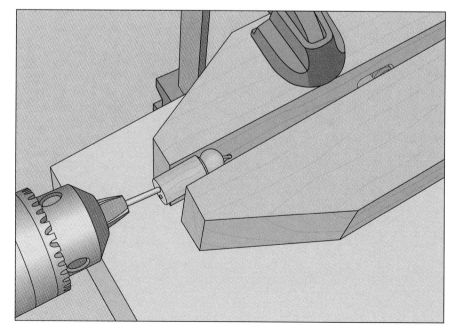

11 Shaping the helmet

Use a spindle sander to shape the nutcracker's helmet. To produce the design shown at right, remove waste wood from three sides of the stock, sanding each side a little at a time to help keep the design symmetrical. Other helmet shapes are shown in the color photo on page 130; these helmets were shaped while the head blank was still on the lathe.

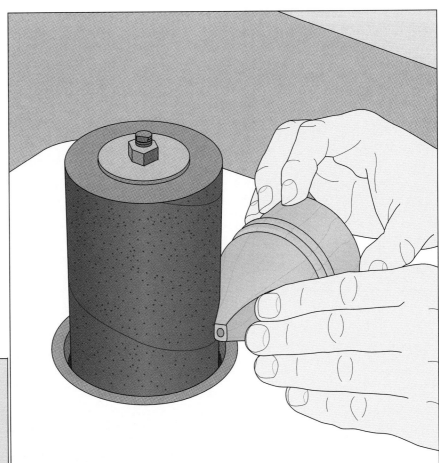

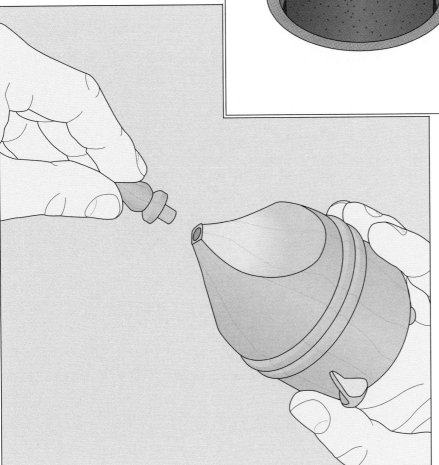

12 Finishing the nutcracker

Turn a finial that crowns the helmet from a ⅝-inch dowel. Include a tenon at the bottom of the finial to fit a matching hole in the helmet, then glue the pieces together *(left)*. To attach the head to the torso, drill matching holes in their contacting surfaces and glue in dowels to secure the connection. Finish by assembling the arms and carving the nose and belt buckle. You can also add details to the nutcracker's uniform, including buttons, epaulet trim, an insignia and trouser leg trim.

WHITE CEDAR BIRD

A marvel of green woodworking, the white cedar bird shown in this section seems to defy logic. Made from a single piece of cedar, its wing feathers form a 3 ¼-inch-wide fan that stays in place without a single drop of glue.

Using a technique developed by the late Chester Nutting, Edmond Menard of Cabot, Vermont, crafted the white cedar bird shown at left. Sliced from a single block of fresh wood, the bird's feathers spread out easily when the wood is wet, but lock into place when the wood dries. Menard has made more than 50,000 birds since 1976; he can carve a bird in under 10 minutes.

The key to success with this technique is to use freshly cut white cedar, which is pliable as long as it stays moist. Start preparing the bird blanks as soon as possible after the tree has been felled. Buck the tree into 18-inch lengths, square up the log on the jointer, and cut it into ½-inch-thick strips on your band saw. Next, move to the table saw and rip the strips 1 inch wide and crosscut them into 8-inch lengths—enough for two birds. If you prepared more blanks than you can use right away, wrap them in plastic and store them in the freezer.

The only remaining tool needed for this project is a sharp shop knife, used to notch the feather shape and slice the individual feathers, and a scroll saw to cut the profile of the bird.

CRAFTING A CEDAR BIRD

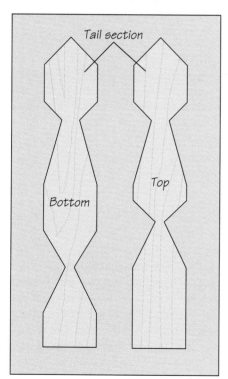

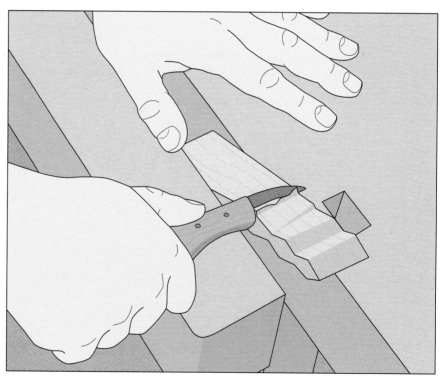

1 Carving the blank to shape

Trace the profiles of the bird *(above, left)* on the top and bottom of your blank. Draw lines along the sides to connect the transition points. The notches in the tail section will allow the individual feathers to interlock, as shown in step 4.

Once the outlines are done, secure the blank with one side facing up in a bench vise. Use a shop knife to slice away waste to the marked outlines, cutting away from your body *(above, right)*.

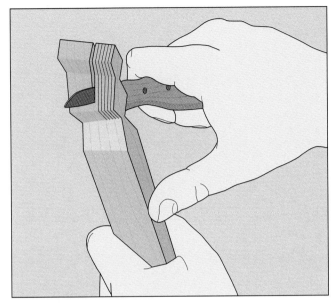

2 Splitting out the tail feathers

Use a sharp knife to slice the tail section of the blank into feathers. Holding the blank firmly, pull the blade squarely into the end grain, cutting slices of about ½₂ inch thick *(above)*. Stop the cut when you reach the body section of the blank. Since you are cutting toward your hand, push the blade slowly and carefully through the wood. Once you have shaved halfway through the thickness of the blank, turn it over and work toward the middle from the other side. You may need to snap off a feather near the tail's center to make room for the blade as the pieces begin to spread. With a 1-inch-wide blank, you should be able to produce about 30 feathers.

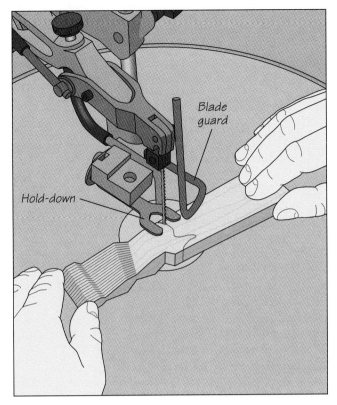

3 Cutting the profile

Once all the feathers are cut, outline the front of the bird on the blank, then cut it out on your scroll saw. To keep the workpiece from chattering, press it against the saw table with hold-down *(above)*. Use the knife to finish the shaping. Proceed quickly to the next step while the wood is wet and pliable.

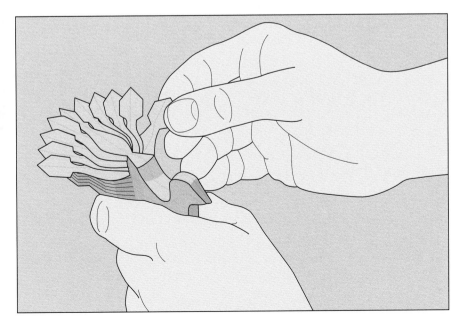

4 Spreading the wings

Starting at the top of the bird, spread the second feather to one side and tuck its arrowhead-shaped end over the top feather. Repeat with the next feather below, but spread it to the other side. Continue in this manner, spreading the feathers outward *(left)* and tucking their ends over the previous feather. To complete the project, you can burn in eyes, a mouth, and marks on the tail feathers. Once the wood has dried, finish the bird with a single, light coat of shellac.

HAND MIRROR

Practical and elegant, hand mirrors like those shown in this section are relatively simple to make, but you will have to devote some time to setting up. The first step is to decide the diameter of the mirror glass; 5-inch beveled glass works well, but other sizes are available. You will then need to produce two templates for laying out the mirror on your stock: one for the shape of the mirror body and a round one for the diameter of the glass recess. Use clear acrylic plastic for both templates to enable you to see the grain and figure of the wood as you locate the outline on your blanks. Make the mirror from ⅝-inch-thick stock. To cut the recess for the glass, use a router paired with a plywood template. Fitted with a straight bit and a template guide, the router will duplicate the template's profile on the workpiece. The recess should be ⅛ inch larger than the glass to allow for wood movement. Make the template long enough to allow you to clamp it in place without interfering with the router.

Ergonomically designed to fit comfortably in the hand, the mirrors shown above can be made from solid wood or, like the sample on the right, from laminated strips of contrasting species. Both were made by Ken Picou, of Austin, Texas.

MAKING A HAND MIRROR

1 Outlining the mirror body
Design your mirror on a piece of acrylic plastic and cut it out as a template on the band saw. Then set the template on your mirror body blank with the length of the mirror parallel to the grain of the blank; position the template to best accentuate the grain and figure of the wood. Outline the template on the stock with a pencil *(right)*. Repeat with the template for the glass recess.

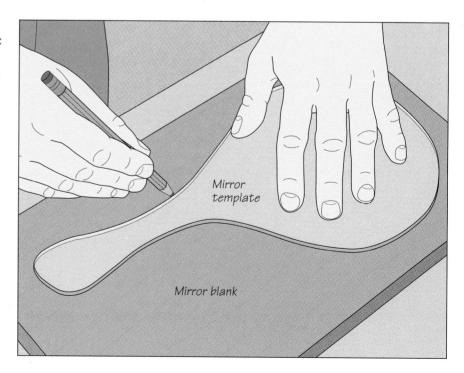

Mirror template

Mirror blank

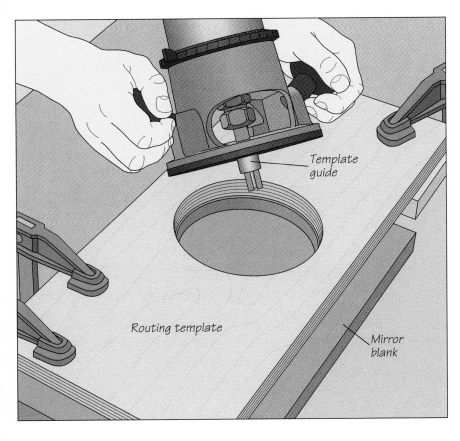

Template guide

Routing template

Mirror blank

2 Routing the recess

To make the routing template, outline the recess on a piece of plywood and add the diameter of the template guide, then cut the hole on a scroll saw or router. Set the mirror blank on a work surface and clamp the template on top, centering the hole over the recess outline. Adjust the router to cut a ⅜-inch-deep recess, then plunge the bit into the stock until the base plate is flat on the template. Ride the template guide along the edge of the template to define the perimeter of the recess, then move the router in small clockwise circles to clear the remaining waste. If you are working with hard wood, you may have to make several passes to reach the final depth.

3 Cutting the mirror body

Once the recess is done, cut out the mirror body on your band saw, keeping both hands clear of the blade *(above)*. Sand the edges, then use a table-mounted router fitted with a round-over bit to shape the edges. Fix the glass to the body with clear silicone adhesive.

SHOP TIP

Making laminated-wood hand mirrors
Hand mirrors made from laminated strips of contrasting wood add visual flair to the final product and are fairly simple to make. Start with two contrasting blanks about ¾ inch thick. Place one on top of the other and temporarily bond the pieces face to face with a drop of epoxy at each corner. Draw the mirror pattern on the top piece, then cut it out through both blanks on your band saw. Carefully pry the pieces apart and simply glue them back together, bonding the central portion of each blank with the outside pieces of the other. To allow for the saw blade kerf, you can also add a strip of veneer to each glue joint.

GLOSSARY

A-B-C

Aliphatic glue: A strong, all-purpose glue ideal for bonding porous surfaces; withstands humidity and heat well.

Bead: A convex shape turned in spindle work; see *cove*.

Bench dog: A round or square peg made of metal or wood that fits into a hole in a workbench to hold a workpiece in place.

Bending form: A jig used to bend steamed or laminated wood.

Bevel cut: A cut at an angle from face to face along the length or width of a workpiece; see *miter cut*.

Box joint: Identical interlocking fingers that mesh to form a corner joint.

Caul: A board placed between clamps and the workpiece to distribute clamping pressure.

Chuck: An accessory mounted in the headstock or tailstock of a lathe to hold a blank for turning.

Clearance hole: A hole bored in a workpiece to accommodate the shank of a screw; see *counterbore hole* and *countersink hole*.

Counterbore hole: A hole drilled into a workpiece permitting the head of a screw or bolt to sit below the wood surface so that it can be concealed by a wood plug.

Countersink hole: A hole drilled into a workpiece that allows a screw head to lie flush with or slightly below the surface.

Cove: A concave decorative profile cut in wood, usually along an edge; see *bead*.

Cross dowel connector: A knock-down fastener that accepts a bolt or screw, typically used to reinforce a butt joint involving an end-grain surface.

D-E-F-G-H-I

Dado: A rectangular channel cut across the grain of a workpiece.

Downhill cutting: In spindle work on the lathe, cutting with the grain rather than against it; working across the grain from a high point to a low.

Escutcheon: A decorative fitting installed around a keyhole to prevent damage to the surrounding wood by the key.

Faceplate turning: A turning technique in which the grain of the workpiece is perpendicular to the lathe's axis; the workpiece is usually only mounted to the headstock of the machine. See *spindle turning*.

Featherboard: A board with thin fingers or "feathers" along one end, clamped to the fence or table of a stationary tool to hold the workpiece securely.

Feed rate: The speed at which a workpiece is pushed into the blade or cutters of a woodworking machine, or the rate at which a tool is pushed into a workpiece.

Fingernail grind: The curved shape ground on the edge of a turning gouge; so-called because the profile is similar to the curve on the end of a fingernail.

Flocking: Spraying very fine felt fibers onto a surface coated with an adhesive to simulate suede.

Grain: The arrangement and direction of the fibers that make up wood.

Headstock: The fixed end of a lathe incorporating the drive spindle; connected to the motor by one or more drive belts.

Inlay: A decorative strip of metal, wood, or marquetry that is glued into a groove cut into a workpiece.

J-K-L-M-N-O-P-Q

Jacobs chuck: A three-jaw chuck used to hold small turning work in the headstock or drilling attachments in the tailstock of a lathe.

Jig: A device for guiding a tool or holding a workpiece in position.

Jointing: Cutting thin shavings from the surface of a workpiece until it is flat and perpendicular to the adjoining surface.

Kerf: The cut made by a saw blade.

Laminate bending: Bending wood by resawing into thin, flexible strips and then gluing up the strips around a curved form.

Lathe capacity: The maximum length and diameter of workpieces that can be mounted on a lathe.

Lobes and sockets: The interlocking joints used in jigsaw-type puzzles.

Miter cut: A cut that angles across the face of a workpiece; see *bevel cut.*

Mortise-and-tenon: A joinery technique in which a projecting tenon on one board fits into a cavity—the mortise—in another.

Parting tool: A cutting tool used primarily to make sizing cuts on the lathe and part off workpieces.

Pilot hole: A hole bored into a workpiece to accommodate a nail shaft or the threaded part of a screw; usually slightly smaller than the fastener diameter. The hole guides the fastener and prevents splitting.

Pilot bearing: A cylindrical metal collar either above or below the router's bit that rides along the workpiece or a template, guiding the bit during the cut.

Plate joint: A method of joining wood using oval wafers of compressed wood that fit into slots cut in mating boards.

Push block or stick: A device used to feed a workpiece into the blade, cutter, or bit of a tool to protect the operator's fingers.

R-S

Rabbet: A step-like cut in the edge or end of a workpiece; usually forms part of a joint.

Roughing gouge: A lathe tool usually used to turn a square blank into a cylinder.

Sizing cuts: A cut to a specific depth made with a parting tool on a lathe.

Skew chisel: A lathe cutting tool with an angled cutting edge beveled on both sides; used to make basic and decorative spindle cuts.

Soss hinge: The trade name for a type of cylindrical hinge that is concealed in mortises in mating workpieces.

Spindle gouge: A turning tool with a curved cutting edge beveled to 30° used for cutting beads and coves and for general spindle work.

Spindle turning: A turning technique in which the grain of the workpiece is parallel to the lathe's axis; the workpiece is held between centers in the tailstock and headstock. Also known as turning between centers. See *faceplate turning.*

Stop block: A block of wood clamped to the fence or miter gauge of a stationary tool to enable a workpiece to be positioned properly for repeat cuts.

Strike plate: A metal plate attached to a door or box frame that engages the the bolt or latch of a doorknob or key.

Substrate: A piece of plywood or solid wood used as a core in veneering or laminating.

T-U-V-W-X-Y-Z

Taper cut: A sloping cut on a spindle turning that decreases its thickness at one end.

Tearout: The ragged edges produced when a blade or cutter tears the wood fibers rather than cutting them cleanly.

Template: A pattern, typically made of plywood or hardboard, used with a power tool to produce multiple copies of an original.

Ultra-high molecular weight plastic (UHMW): Very dense, long-wearing plastic that can be fastened in strips.

INDEX

Page references in *italics* indicate an illustration of subject matter. Page references in **bold** indicate a Build It Yourself project.

ACKNOWLEDGMENTS

The editors wish to thank the following:

TOYS AND CRAFTS BASICS
Delta International Machinery/Porter-Cable, Guelph, Ont.; Health And Welfare Canada
(Product Safety Division), Longueuil, Que.; Record Tools Inc., Pickering, Ont.;
Chester Van Ness, Scotland, Ont.; Woodcraft Supply Corp., Parkersburg, WV

MODELS
Adjustable Clamp Co., Chicago, IL; Black & Decker/Elu Power Tools, Towson, MD;
Delta International Machinery/Porter-Cable, Guelph, Ont.; Garnet Hall, Stoughton, Sask.;
Doug Kenney, South Dennis, MA; Tool Trend Ltd., Concord, Ont.; Chester Van Ness, Scotland, Ont.

SLEIGHS AND SLEDS
Adjustable Clamp Co., Chicago, IL; A.J. Douglas Angus, Richmond, BC; Delta International
Machinery/Porter-Cable, Guelph, Ont.; Mike Dunbar, Portsmouth, NH; Walter Last, Winnipeg, Man.;
Jean-Pierre Masse, Montreal, Que.; Norway Nordic, Ste-Anne-de-Bellevue, Que.; Ryobi America Corp.,
Anderson, SC; Sears, Roebuck and Co., Chicago, IL; John Sollinger, North Ferrisburg, VT;
Steiner/Lamello A.G. Switzerland/Colonial Saw Co., Kingston, MA; Tool Trend Ltd., Concord, Ont.

ROCKING HORSES
Adjustable Clamp Co., Chicago, IL; Don Buhler, Swan River, Man.; Delta International
Machinery/Porter Cable, Guelph, Ont.; Great Neck Saw Mfrs. Inc. (Buck Bros. Division),
Millbury, MA; Ryobi America Corp., Anderson, SC; Fred Sneath, Woodview, Ont.

DOLLHOUSES
Adjustable Clamp Co., Chicago, IL; Canplay/Kitchener Importers, Ajax, Ont.; Delta International
Machinery/Porter-Cable, Guelph, Ont.; Greenleaf Products Incorporated, Honeyoye Falls, NY;
Hobby World, Montreal, Que.; Carlo Zappa, Montreal, Que.

GAMES AND PUZZLES
Adjustable Clamp Co., Chicago, IL; Black & Decker/Elu Power Tools, Towson, MD; Delta International
Machinery/Porter-Cable, Guelph, Ont.; DonJer Products Corp., Belle Mead, NJ; Ray Levy, Soquel, CA;
Steve Malavolta, Albuquerque, NM; Michael D. Mode, New Haven, VT; Record Tools Inc., Pickering, Ont.;
Tool Trend Ltd., Concord, Ont.; Woodcraft Supply Corp., Parkersburg, WV

CRAFT CLASSICS
Adjustable Clamp Co., Chicago, IL; American Tool Co., Lincoln, NE; Delta International
Machinery/Porter-Cable, Guelph, Ont.; Great Neck Saw Mfrs. Inc. (Buck Bros. Division), Millbury, MA;
Hitachi Power Tools U.S.A. Ltd., Norcross, GA; David Keller, Petaluma, CA; Edmond Menard, Cabot, VT;
Ken Picou Design, Austin, TX; Record Tools Inc., Pickering, Ont.; Ryobi America Corp., Anderson, SC;
Sears, Roebuck and Co., Chicago, IL; Fred Sneath, Woodview, Ont.; The Home Shop, Charlotte, MI;
Tool Trend Ltd., Concord, Ont.; Woodcraft Supply Corp., Parkersburg, WV

The following persons also assisted in the preparation of this book:

Lorraine Doré, Martin Francoeur, Ruth Karp, Roger Landreville, Rob Lutes, Jim McRae, Bryan Quinn

PICTURE CREDITS

Cover Robert Chartier
6,7 Michael Tincher
8,9 Brian Milne/First Light
10,11 Marie Louise Deruaz
62 Brian Milne/First Light